DIALECTICS OF FREEDOM FOR NIGERIA'S POLITICAL STABILITY

Towards Actualizing Nigerian Political Stability from the
Paradigm of Frantz Fanon's Dialectics of Freedom

EVARISTUS EMEKA ISIFE

authorHOUSE®

AuthorHouse™
1663 Liberty Drive
Bloomington, IN 47403
www.authorhouse.com
Phone: 833-262-8899

Published by AuthorHouse 11/24/2021

ISBN: 978-1-6655-4346-0 (sc)
ISBN: 978-1-6655-4345-3 (e)

CONTENTS

DEDICATION

This work is dedicated to Onye -Nkuzi Stephen Nnachi Isife and Ezinne Evangeline Nkechi Isife, my parents, who first taught me about life and to all my teachers for sowing in me the seed of what I am today.

ACKNOWLEDGEMENTS

I wish to express my sentiments of appreciation to all persons who encouraged and supported me during the course of writing this work. I thank the Almighty God for his grace towards me in spite of my weaknesses. I will never be tired of praying for Most Rev. Prof. Godfery Igwebuike Onah, my bishop, for always playing well his role as a father to me. My deepest thanks go to Assoc. Prof. Ifechi Ndianefo who supervised my master's thesis that provoked this work and all the lecturers in the Department of Philosophy, Faulty of Arts, Nnamdi Azikwie University, Awka, Anambra state.

I thank in a special way all those who supported and helped me towards the completion of this work: Prof. Pat Ngwu, Fr. Prof. Ikechukwu Kanu, Rev. Frs. Dr. Jude Odo, Dr. Anthony Agbilibeazu, Dr. Charles Okoro, Anthony Anichebe, Kevin Nnamchi, Jude Ugwueke, Malachy Ezea, Augustine Anwuchie, Ekene Oguejiofor, to name but a few. I cannot forget the useful and insightful contributions made by Dr. Emeka Greg. Chinweuba, Dr Emmanuel Archibong, Dr. Stan. Unodiaku, Engr. Matthew Odo, Matthew Ihondu and Osinachi Ochei. I also appreciate my parents, Mr Stephen and Mrs Evangeline Isife, and my siblings: Okey, Ifeanyi, Onyeka and Uju, for always being there for me. I thank Fr. Dr. Humphery Uche Ani, the head of Department of Philosophy, Bigard Memorial Seminary Enugu, for not only writing the foreword to this work but also for his useful suggestions towards making the work what it is. I also thank Dr. Ejikemeuwa Ndubuisi, who wrote the preface of this book. Finally, I thank the old boys, staff and students of Corpus Christi College Achi, the people of God of St. Micheal's Egwu Achi and Holy Redeemer Parish Nru- Nsukka, the priests of Awgu and Nsukka Dioceses and the family of Bigard Memorial Seminary Enugu for contributing to making me what I am today. May the almighty God bless and protect you all.

FOREWORD

Intellectual instrument is one of the principal tools used by the colonial masters to perpetuate their control of the conquered territories. It was a strong weapon that helped to tame, in the name of teaching, the mind and heart of the colonized. This was very much challenged when the colonized became conscious of this subtle chain on their psyche. Among Africans and Africans in Diaspora, the realization of the fact that their minds were ruled by what they were taught and made to believe became the turning point in their revolution for a better life. In the face of Eurocentric ideologies and Western intellectualism, Afrocentrists have responded in robust expressions in various ways to checkmate the social and mind control of the Africans by the colonizers. This historic challenge against occidental domineering scholarship was championed by the likes of Cheikh Anta Diop, Leopold Sedar Senghor, Aime Césaire, Molefi Asante and Innocent Onyewuenyi. Their struggles ignited a course for new energy on African studies, of which the indices as seen in the birth of movements like Negritude or Afrocentrism became rallying cry against the European colonists and Eurocentric intellectualism.

The rise of Africanist scholars energised new intellectual movements in history and philosophy whose aim was to enervate the erroneous historical reason that has been perpetuated by European scholars against Africa and Africans. Its development provided a platform against the attempts to build an intellectual rationale with the aim at justifying the political actions of Westerners and the forceful impositions of their concepts and values on other societies they consider inferior. The emergence of eminent African intellectuals, historians, activists, critics and philosophers whose ideas provoked and spurred revolutions of perception and active rejection of colonized personality, sought in the same vein to redefine the social identity and liberty of the African. One of the most vocal of these pacesetters of African freedom in the mission for redemption of the African identity and personality was Frantz Fanon. Fanon used his erudite scholarship to resist imperialist intellectualism and political intimidation of the Africans by the White colonizers, and demanded that the reversion of the ugly elements in world history against Blacks needs to happen. This is the central message of his reflections on the dialectics of freedom. He motivated Africans to assert themselves against their unjust aggressors by every means available to them. In decades later, this will become the source of inspiration for liberation and rejection of oppression by every available means that can be explored by the Africans.

The reflections of Fanon on the dialectics of freedom created a stimulus, not only for the liberation of Africans from European colonizers, but have become the source of force to fight the internally generated African despots and "colonizers" against Africans. This is why the author of this work, Fr. Evaristus Emeka Isife has decided to tap on the Fanonian genius in his own effort to inspire a liberation of Nigerians and Africans from the oppression and exploitation of their home-made despots and political traitors who have consistently starved the people of good governance and equitable distribution of common good and democratic dividends in Africa. As he clearly captures this Fanonian thesis: "dialectics of freedom is an anti-colonial philosophical thought relevant not only for curbing racism but conscious exploitation and hindrance of peoples' socio-economic advancement as well as socio-political equality in human societies". In this thought-provoking work, he engages the reader with deep discussions on the notion and values of the dialectics of freedom in the struggle and survival of the oppressed, especially in Africa. He re-equips the struggling African with the Fanonian options in the post-colonial demand for justice and social equity.

The Chapter one of this work explains the essential terms upon which the reflections of the author revolve. It gives explanations on such terms as dialectics, freedom, paradigm shift, political instability, colonization and violence. From Chapter Two to Six, the author provides deep insight on the salient points of Fanon's discussion on freedom. He delved into the roots of the Fanonian concept of freedom, the major scholarly influences that shaped his discussions on the notion. He identified the role of the dialectics of the Manicheans, Hegel and Marx in the formation of the dialectics on which the revolutionary necessity of the oppressed for their liberation is built. However, he remarked that Fanon's dialectics took a precise focus on the oppressed Africans, who were colonized by the Whites. The attitude of the colonizer according to him created the thesis which made the anti-thesis of violence in the oppressed inevitable. It is hoped that such necessary anti-thesis is the only basis for a possible emergence of freedom that can guarantee an equitable and balanced relationship among races and classes of people in the human society.

In the remaining chapters of the work, the author analyzes the Nigerian chequered political history, both civilian and military, which is tainted with much illustrations of oppression by "internal" colonization of Blacks by Blacks. He hopes that the Fanonian dialectics of freedom can clean the Augean stable of the Nigerian political disorder and impunity. The Fanonian concept of freedom which means revolution against the oppressor, aims at restoring equal humanity for all and intends to serve as viable paradigm shift towards a creative and lasting freedom for all. This means a recognition of the responsibility by all to topple the bad governance in Nigeria, and a restoration of integrity and humanity to the deprived and the oppressed Nigerians. This will become the real birth of political independence of the Nigerian people. In this book therefore, the author offers a clear insight through the political philosophy of Frantz Fanon, for the anthropological and social emancipation of the oppressed everywhere, and Nigerians in particular. It provides the right sense and stimulus for all seeking political and social liberty and equality. It is a masterpiece as well as a deep reflection on the underlining precepts which can guide a genuine seeker of freedom, to find his goal. It is an academic manifesto as well as a social agenda for the oppressed who earnestly seek liberty, dignity, integrity, and indeed, fullness of humanity.

Rev. Fr. Dr. Humphrey Uchenna Ani,
Head of Philosophy Department,
Bigard Memorial Seminary,
Enugu.

PREFACE

Experience has shown that every being has some fundamental structures that account for the existence of a particular being. The unity of a being goes a long way to portray the identity of that particular being. Our knowledge of transcendental properties of being in metaphysics shows that a being is to the extent that it is one. So, oneness or unity is an essential character of a being. A particular being loses its identity if it lacks the essential unity of its being. Violence is a serious threat to the unity of being especially as regards human society. This explains why our author, wearing the lens of Frantz Fanon, argues that the human person has to do everything possible to counter anything that attempts to dehumanize the being of the human person either as individual or as a group. This is the central message of this book: *DIALECTICS OF FREEDOM FOR NIGERIAN POLITICAL STABILITY: Towards actualizing Nigerian Political Stability from the Paradigm of Frantz Fanon's Dialectics of Freedom.*

The book in your hands is a product of a well-researched work by an African scholar who is bent on sustaining the identity of the African person and African nations with particular reference to Nigeria. Our author, Rev. Fr. Evaristus Emeka Isife, is of the view that the present political structure engendered by the colonial masters constitute a serious threat to the being called Nigeria. And so, in the line of thought of Frantz Fanon, he argues that the human person cannot fully realise himself / herself while in a bondage of any sort. There is need for political and economic freedom. It is in an atmosphere of freedom that one can say to have fully realized one's potentialities. Violence, as conceived by Fanon, is not an end in itself but a means to an end. This violence is creative violence against the oppressors; it is such a violence that is geared towards liberation. For Fanon, mere violence, without a clear plan for decolonization and liberation, would only reproduce the power relations of the colonizer.

What we know today as Nigeria came into being in 1914 with the amalgamation of the Southern and Northern Protectorates. This was made possible under the governorship of Sir Frederick Lugard. The union of the two protectorates gave rise to a new sociopolitical structure for the new country – Nigeria. This is an existential fact. Nigeria, as it is today, requires overhauling of its structures in order to engender both individual freedom and national freedom. The present Nigerian structures are not actually in the best interest of Nigeria. Some of the structures are such that they promote disunity, tribalism, mediocrity, unproductivity, laziness, discrimination, among others. The major point here, as argued by our author, is that there is need for a holistic sociopolitical restructuring in Nigeria. Nigeria cannot experience authentic existence without proper appreciation and application of freedom as an essential commodity. So, the status quo (thesis) has to be countered (anti-thesis) and this will lead us to a restructured society (synthesis). This is the dialectics of freedom in sum.

This book is quite interesting and thought-provoking. You cannot but applaud at the end of each chapter because of the ingenuity and mastery exhibited by our author. This is a book that has the capacity to bring about the desired positive change needed for the political stability of Nigeria. Those within the corridors of power should endeavour to read and digest the content of this book. Lecturers, students, researchers, and in fact, all lovers of freedom will find in this book a repository of knowledge and an essential tool for action.

Ejikemeuwa J. O. Ndubisi, PhD
Associate Professor of Philosophy
Department of Philosophy
Tansian University, Umunya, Nigeria

CHAPTER ONE

INTRODUCTION

1.1 NIGERIA'S POOR POLITICAL CONDITION AND FANON'S REMEDY

Nigerian political development is characterized by political instability. This is as a result of the inherited colonial pattern of authority that has become the trend of politics and governance. Because this colonial pattern does not cohere with the autochthonous political interpretations and cultural understanding of politics and governance by indigenous Nigerian people, it has remained the fulcrum of unabated political instability in Nigeria. The result has been poor and predatory governance, collapse of critical sectors, infrastructural decay and deficiency, unemployment, mass poverty, violent agitations, terrorism and conflict. Political instability has indeed defied leadership strategies of successive governments and well-meaning Nigerians. As such, not only is the very existence of Nigeria threatened, political development sets those in government against the people as it reflects a kind of colonialism in which the masses are dominated, exploited and dehumanized. It is on this note that Fanon's anti-colonial philosophy, represented as dialectics of freedom, remains central in the pursuit of Nigerian liberation and true freedom.

In remedy to Nigerian political instability therefore is Fanon's dialectics of freedom which can serve as a viable paradigm shift towards human liberation and true freedom. This is as Fanon's dialectics of freedom hinges on avenues to true human and national freedom, sustainable development and stability. Dialectics of freedom is an anti-colonial philosophical thought relevant not only for curbing racism but conscious exploitation and hindrance of peoples' socio-economic advancement as well as socio-political equality in human societies.[1]

Although, this philosophical thought was born of Fanon's commitment to Algerian decolonization struggle, it remains relevant "in salvaging contemporary African states from the present neocolonial influences, domination and exploitations."[2] As such, post-colonial Nigeria is only different from the colonial past based on the fact that indigenous Nigerians replaced the

---

[1] Jinadu Adele, *Fanon: In Search of the African Revolution* (Enugu: Fourth Dimension Publishers, 1980), 21-22.
[2] Evaristus Emeka Isife, "Dialectics of Freedom in Frantz Fanon and its Relevance in Contemporary Africa," in *IGWEBUIKE: An African Journal of Arts and Humanities*, vol. 6, no. 9, (2020): 119.

European colonists[3]. In reality, the predatory contents and principles of colonialism remain the order of politics and governance. This is more so as these indigenous stooges now exploit their own people to their advantages, those of their cronies and western masters. Thus, the larger Nigerian population is still captive, exploited and dehumanized. In this situation, the oppressed quest for true freedom is still crystallized in Fanon's dialectics of freedom. The motion of this dialectic gains momentum through self-consciousness of the oppressed. For, this consciousness stands as the antithesis of the exploitative and dehumanising order leading to a better human condition.

Indeed, the being of the oppressors and oppressed is reflected in Fanonian Manichean colonial world.[4] This is a world of clash of interests between the projected evil and the self-acclaimed good. As such, there is bound to be clash between oppressors that claimed to be embodiment of universal good and the oppressed that are projected to be evil. The resultant synthesis in the light of Fanon's is the new order reflecting liberation and true freedom of the dominated and oppressed. This is why Fanon's dialectics of freedom remains a systematic movement of freedom from contradictory societal circumstances to its original and better form.

1.2 OUTSTANDING TERMS IN THIS DISCOURSE

1.2.1 *Dialecticss*

The word "dialectics" is a method of investigating or discussing the truth of opinion. Some of the earliest examples of the dialectics are the *Dialogues* of Plato, in which the author sought to study truth through discussion in the form of questions and answers. Another notable Greek philosopher Aristotle thought of dialectics as the search for the philosophical basis of science. He frequently used the term as a synonym for the science of logic. The German philosopher, George Wilhelm Fredrische Hegel applied the term *dialectics* in his philosophical thoughts. This is because Hegel believed that evolution of ideas occurs through dialectical process – that is, when a concept (the thesis) gives rise to its opposite (the antithesis) and as a result of this conflict, a third concept, (the synthesis), arises. In dialectics, the synthesis is a higher level of truth than the thesis and the antithesis.

Hegel's work is based on the idealistic concept of a universal mind glaring in the conception that true evolution arrives at the highest level of self-awareness and freedom. But the most familiar understanding of Hegel's dialectics is seen as a process of thought by which apparent contradictions (which are termed as the thesis and antithesis) are seen to be part of a higher truth (synthesis)[5]. Thus, Hegel describes the movement of consciousness in self-realisation as dialectical movement in which each mode of consciousness in realising itself in a higher form is negated.

Marx adopts this dialectic which is glaring in negation, but converts the abstract movement

---

[3] Ikechukwu Onah, *The Battle of Democracy: Social Justice and Punishment in Africa* (Enugu : Fidgina Global Books, 2006),18.

[4] La Rose T. Parris, "Frantz Fanon: Existentialist, Dialectician, and Revolutionary," in *The Journal of Pan African Studies*, vol. 4, no. 7,(2011):6.

[5] Simon Blackburn, *Oxford Dictionary of Philosophy* (Oxford: Oxford University Press, 2008), 301 – 02.

of Hegel's Absolute Spirit (which forms Hegel's dialectics) into movement of human praxis. In other words, Marx translates Hegel's concern for the Absolute Spirit into that of man's relation with nature and to each other.[6] Despite this, the popular meaning of dialectics as movements of two opposing positions or ideas towards a better position or ideas as represented by thesis, antithesis and synthesis remains. But unlike Marx, who believes in the inevitable and objective dialectics of material forces in the historical process without the freedom of man shaping events, Fanon maintains that the transcendence and freedom of man is the dialectics of man with the environment and with each other in the historical process. In this way, Fanon holds that Man is free and therefore responsible for the creation of socio-political order at the present and the future.

1.2.2 Freedom

Freedom is the quality of being free, in other words, absence of necessity, coercion or constraint in choice or action. It is the power or condition of acting without compulsion and restraint. Freedom can also be defines as :

> self-determination, self-control, self-direction, self regulation. The ability of an agent to act or not to act according to his dictates. Being able to act in conformity with that which one wills. Being the cause of one's own action. The ability to choose and the opportunity to satisfy or procure that choice.[7]

Freedom can as well mean liberation from slavery, quality or state of being exempted from something onerous, quality of being frank, open or outspoken. Here, there is a strong relationship between freedom and liberation. Both of them mean the power or condition of acting without compulsion. Freedom has a broad range of application from total absence of restraint to merely a sense of not being unduly hampered or frustrated. Liberty suggests a release from former restraint or compulsion. Based on these, freedom and liberation are employed interchangeably in this discourse. With these meanings, this treatise bothers more on political freedom, that is, freedom from oppression or coercion, absence of disenabling conditions for an individual or absence of life condition of compulsion. Although political freedom is often interpreted negatively as freedom from unreasonable external constraint or action; such freedom can also reflect in positive exercise of social or group rights, capacities and action.[8] This is why Fanon's dialectics of freedom anchors on releasing possibilities of human existence and history imprisoned by the colonization of experience and the racialisation of consciousness.[9]

---

[6] Richard Onwuanibe, *A Critique of Revolutionary Humanism: Frantz Fanon* (USA: Warren H. Green Inc., 1983), 18.

[7] Kevin C. Arua, "Man is Free to be Free and not Free not to be Free," in *UCHE: Journal of the Department of Philosophy, University of Nigeria Nsukka*, vol. 13, (2007):2.

[8] Charles Taylor, "What's Wrong with Negative Liberty?" in *Philosophy and the Human Science: Philosophical Papers* (Cambridge: Cambridge University Press, 1985):229.

[9] Otu Ato–Sekyi, *Fanon's Dialectic of Experience* (London: Harvard University Press, 1996), 5.

1.2.3 *Paradigm*

The term paradigm was first introduced and used in philosophy of science by Thomas Kuhn. This use was reflected in the first edition of his book, *The Structure of Scientific Revolution* (1962). Thus it is from Kuhn that "the use of the term 'paradigm' become firmly entrenched as a standard expression in English and appears in cartoons and business management courses, although most of the contemporary users have no notion of its source."[10] Kuhn understands paradigm to be a universal recognized scientific achievement, which for a time provides model problems and solution for community of practitioners. He maintains that the term 'paradigm' is used in two different senses.

On the more general sense, it stands for the entire constellation of beliefs, values, and techniques shared by the members of a given community. In a narrower sense, it denotes one sort of element in that constellation; the concrete puzzle–solutions which when employed as models or examples can replace explicit rules as a basis for the solution of the remaining puzzles of normal science[11].

Moreover, Kuhn defined the two kinds of scientific development in terms of paradigms. One is normal science which involves the articulation and refinement of a paradigm that is shared by the relevant scientific community. The other is revolutionary science that involves the rejection of one paradigm and replacement with another.[12] Along this line, there is a distinction between the colonial paradigm, which is likened to the normal science and the anti–colonial paradigm, which is likened to the revolutionary science. It is in this sense that this work uses paradigm as a standard that should be either jettisoned or accepted.

Fanon has said it *ab initio* that his theory of freedom, although built from his experiences in Martinique, France and Algeria, can serve as a paradigm for struggle for freedom in other African countries.[13] So, his discussions on freedom of Africa revolve around two themes: the central guiding role played by Algeria and the Algerian Revolution in Africa and the need for concentrated efforts to oust France and Europe from the continent. At the conferences held in Accra and Monrovia in 1958, and at every conference held in Africa that involved countries of Black Africa as well as the Maghreb, Fanon always raised the Algerian question and had always projected the Algerian revolution as a paradigm for the continent of Africa.[14] The high point of this book is therefore to demonstrate how dialectics of freedom in Frantz Fanon can serve as a paradigm for political stability in Nigeria.

---

[10] Ifechukwu Ndianefoo, *A Critical History of Philosophy of Science* (Awka: Divine Press, 2016), 321.

[11] Thomas Kuhn, "The Structure of Scientific Revolution" in *International Encyclopedia of Unified Science* edited by Otto Neurath et al., (London: The University of Chicago Press Ltd, 1970),175.

[12] Ifechi Ndianefoo. 321.

[13] Frantz Fanon, *Black Skin, White Masks*, trans. Charles Lam Markmann (London: Pluto Press, 2008), 5.

[14] Irene Gendzier, *Frantz Fanon: A Critical Study* (London: Wild Wood House Ltd, 1972),188.

1.2.4 Political Instability

The Adjective "political" derives from the noun "politics" which deals the set of activities that are associated with decisions in groups, or other forms of power relations between individuals. It means a fixed or regular system or administration of government relating to civil government and its administration, state affairs and national measures as well as nations/states as distinguished from civil or municipal politics or government.[15] The word "instability" on the other hand has to do with the quality of being unstable, unfixed or not firm in position and discontinuance in the same state because of change. Thus, political instability is a concept used to depict uncertain public affairs of a country. It points to the fluctuating condition of different people's powers and their exercise in a group, organization or country.

Political instability is therefore the quality of unstable state of affairs in governance of a country. In this sense, political instability means a shaky, unsteady, tottering, wobbling and unsafe condition within the governance of a state. This further implies that political instability is a situation not held or fixed securely; a degeneration of political structure which is visible in precarious condition and societal upheavals. Based on this, some scholars view political instability as incidence of political upheaval or violence in society, such as demonstrations, agitations, workers' strike, dissidence, etc. Thus, any uncertain or fluctuating condition in an organization or government as well as the responsive upset from the people amounts to political instability. Seen in this light, political instability depicts an unhealthy condition in a civil society replete with struggle for power, poor decision making, poor policy implementation and people's show of disapproval. As such, revolution, demonstration, strike, terrorism and public violence are associated with political instability.

1.2.5 Colonisation

Colonisation encapsulates all forms of cultural, economic and political exploitation that developed from Europeans' expansion and influence over the last four hundred years. So, colonization is the process of establishing a colony. It is the policy of extending a nation's authority outside its territory for some gains. Thus, colonization is the attitude of dominating the affairs and implanting of settlements in other territory or country.[16]

---

[15] Harry Clarke and Lucinda Summers, *New Webster's Dictionary of the English Language* (U.S.A: Delan Publishing Inc., 1981), 737.

[16] Edward Said, *Culture and Imperialism* (London: Chatto & Windus, 1993), 40.

1.2.6 *Violence*

Violence is a physical attack, physical abuse, physical struggle against a person or animal, vigorous psychological attack against a person or animal as well as destruction of property or potential property.[17] Therefore, violence has physical and psychological aspects.

---

[17] Robert Audi, "On the Meaning and Justification of Violence," in *Violence : An Award Winning Essays in the Council for Philosophical Studies Competition*, edited Jerome Shaffer (New York: David McKay Company Inc., 1971), 59.

CHAPTER TWO

ROOTS OF FRANTZ FANON'S THOUGHTS ON FREEDOM:

2.1 INFLUENCES OF SCHOLARS

The constraints surrounding human existence make thought on freedom inalienable in the cosmic realm. Hence, numerous postulations abound on human freedom. Among these are diverse theories of philosophers from antiquity to the present on freedom. The idea of freedom however took a new dimension with Hegel and Marx. Hegel locates freedom in the realization or rather the actualization of the Absolute Spirit. But Marx argued that freedom can only come about through liberation from the alienation of labour by capital. These earlier thoughts on freedom had great influences on Frantz Fanon's articulation and advocacy of the freedom of the colonized, especially the black race of the world. These influences were also the catalysts that propelled his postulations on freedom as now understood from different standpoints and perspectives. As such, Fanon has become a different person to different people, a psychoanalyst, philosopher, political analyst, journalist, propagandist, freedom fighter, revolutionary and cultural critic. This is why in the posthumous tribute, "The Homage to Frantz Fanon" in *Prescence Africaine,* Aime Cesaire summarized Fanon's theory of freedom by maintaining that *"Black Skin, White Masks* was the crucial book on the human consequences of colonization and racism, while the *Wretched of the Earth* provided the key to the process of decolonization.[18]"

Furthermore, Jock McCulloch has maintained that there are three influential paradigms around which Fanon's theory is rooted which are: Negritude, Ethno-psychology and African Socialism. He reveals that through exploration of Fanon's response to these paradigms, broad dimension of his theory could be traced and identified. Jock McCulloch equally identified and pinned these paradigms as influencing and reflecting aspects of Fanon's personality. In this sense, negritude influences Fanon's quest for personal identity, African socialism reflects his desire to

---

[18] Cesaire Aime, "The Homage to Frantz Fanon," in *Prescence Africaine*, vol.12, no.40, (1962):131

"return to Africa" and ethno-psychiatry influences his professional training and occupation.[19] However, the deficiency of this division lies in the impossibility of determining when and where each paradigm was exacting an influence on Fanon in the course of the development of his dialectics of freedom.

2.2 THE CRITICAL COMPARISON

With critical comparison, Ato Sekyi - Otu demonstrates that behind Fanon's ideas is Aristotelian logic which became the defining logic of the colonizer-colonized relation. For, obedient to the rules of pure Aristotelian logic, both the colonized and colonizer follow the principle of reciprocal exclusivity.[20] This is despite the fact that the zone where the colonized live is not complementary to the zone inhabited by the colonizers. Thus, the two zones are opposed but not in the service of that higher unity.

Otu however gives Irene Gendzier the credit of recognizing in Fanon's account the category of work. This work according to him, is not the redemptive work of Hegel's bondsman, but the wholly object labour of the servant. Thus, Otu holds that a normative but frustrated Hegelian–Marxist is in many aspects implicit in Fanon's social ontology, and as such, Fanon quite evidently accepted the view of value attributes which is ascribed to human work and even the work of the bondsman. So, Fanon has always referred to the Hegelian slave as one who was himself the object and who finds in his work the source of his liberation. Nevertheless, this normative left-Hegelianism precisely led Fanon to discern in the drama of labour and interaction under conditions of racial bondage an entirely different and indeed heterogeneous story. Otu points out that Fanon is of the opinion that an experience of labour disjoined from the pristine promise of reciprocal recognition is incapable of engendering the possibility of liberation. This is why the struggle for liberation of the blacks will have to take a form altogether different from that of Hegel's slave. The story of Hegel's bondsman ends with a prefiguration of his existential vocation. In contrast to this reformism, the emancipation of the racially subjugated will have to be nothing less than a transfiguration, a radical leap "from one life to another."[21]

Otu again maintains that both Hegel's and Sartre's narratives of social being predicated on relations of reciprocity, being or malignant are incapable of capturing the originality of the colonial context. However, Sartre according to Otu has dismissed Hegel's dialectics of reciprocity as totalitarian, and has vetoed the epistemological optimism which dreams of an experience totally shared by the ego and the other, but he has upon the foundation of his own ontology proposed a negative dialectics of reciprocity, which requires that the dependent consciousness be capable of transcending its reduction to the status of a thing by exchanging roles with the independent

---

[19] Jock McCulloch, *Black Soul White Artifact: Fanon's Clinical Psychology and Social Theory* (New York: Cambridge University Press, 2002), 4.

[20] Otu Ato Sekyi, *Fanon's Dialectics of Experience*, 55.

[21] Otu Ato Sekyi, *Fanon's Dialectics of Experience*, 61.

consciousness.[22] But what Fanon retained from Sartre and the existentialists was the formal notion of human liberty as the capability and openness of the field of action and self-determination.

2.3 EVALUATION OF FANON'S HUMANISM

Evaluating the aspect of humanism in Fanon's philosophy, Richard Onwuanibe, in his book, *A Critique of Revolutionary Humanism: Frantz Fanon*, asserts that Fanon's concept of human recognition to a large extent derives from that of Hegel's. The struggle for recognition, from Fanon's perspective, is necessary where there is a challenge to one's humanity. It is at this level that Onwuanibe sees the difference between the master and slave in Hegel's dialectics and the relationship between the white and black or the colonizer and colonized in the colonial context as adumbrated by Fanon. Onwuanibe maintains that the slave in Hegel's analysis is not turned to the master but only aspires to a lower kind of recognition of service, which is not grounded on true independence and freedom. But the black man or the colonized in his relation to the white man or the colonizer wants to be accorded human dignity grounded on independence and freedom. It is from this perspective that one sees the pivotal point of Fanon's humanism in the duality of human negativity which Fanon denotes as yes and no. This duality according to Onwuanibe, is "reflected in his search for recognition through revolution."[23]

On the dialectical character of Fanon's theory of freedom however, Onwuanibe argues that Fanon derives his conception of dialectics from Hegel and Marx with whom the concept is often associated today, though the term "dialectic" has taken on various meaning since Plato. According to Onwuanibe:

> Fanon operates within a dialectical frame work in which the principle of self-defense reinforced by the principle of double effect operates in the achievement of the reconciliation between humanism and violence. In a certain sense, within his dialectical frame work that his humanism is reconciled with violence in a dialectical tension.[24]

Consequently, self-defense violence on the part of the colonized becomes a necessary dialectical response to the thesis of colonization. This book emphasizes more on the dialectical character of Fanon's theory of freedom which has to do with the movement of the two opposing positions of the colonizer and the colonized in the colonial situation towards the synthesis of freedom. So, dialectics of freedom can be described as "Fanon's interpretation of these movements, as demonstrated in his account of the relations between the colonizer and the colonized in the colonial situation."[25] The Hegelian definition of dialectics is a sure guide to appreciating the

---

[22] Otu Ato Sekyi, *Fanon's Dialectics of Experience*,64.

[23] Richard Onwuanibe, *A Critique of Revolutionary Humanism: Frantz Fanon* (U.S.A: Warren H. Green Inc., 1983), 18.

[24] Richard Onwuanibe,431.

[25] Evaristus Emeka Isife. "Dialectics of Freedom in Frantz Fanon: A Potent Tool towards Achieving Political Stability in Nigeria," in *The International Journal of Humanities & Social Studies*, vol. 8, no.5, (2020): 267.

dialectics of freedom in Fanon. The attitude or action of the colonizer is seen as the thesis, that of the colonized as antithesis and relations between the two as the synthesis that would eventually lead to freedom as the two positions are transcended to create a new humanity.

However, Fanon deviates from Hegel and Marx by focusing his theory of freedom on colonization of Africa by the European countries. The slave-owner's strategy of dehumanization, degradation, and depersonalization is similar to that which colonizers applied in order to construct the colonized African as the other and to legitimize colonial domination and exploitation.[26] Hence Fanon maintains that:

> The originality of the colonial context is the economic reality; inequality and the immense difference of ways of life never come to mask the human realities. When you examine at close quarters the colonial context, it is evident that what parcels out the world is to begin with the fact of belonging to or not belonging to a given race, a given specie.[27]

Sure, the African form of colonization is different from others because it is also a racial colonization. That is why Fanon believed that Hegel's master-slave dialectic is to be re-interpreted, and Marxist analysis should be slightly stretched, in order to explain and situate the African colonial experience. The re-interpretation of Hegel's and slightly stretching of Marxism are evidently seen in the dialectics of freedom which destroys the colonial situation and restores true humanity.

---

[26] Floyd Hayes, "Fanon, Oppression and Resentment: The Black Experience in the United States," in *Fanon: A Critical Reader,* edited by Gordon, L.R., et al. (U.S.A: Blackwell Publishers Inc., 1996),16.

[27] Frantz Fanon, *The Wretched of the Earth,* trans. Constance Farrington (London: Penguin Books, 2001), 30 – 31.

CHAPTER THREE

SCHOLARS OVERVIEW ON FANON'S DIALECTICS OF FREEDOM

3.1 STRUGGLE FOR PERSONAL FREEDOM AND LIBERATION OF HUMAN SOCIETY

An important issue that has concerned scholars is whether Fanon was influenced by struggle for his personal freedom or by his concern for the liberation of his society or by both. Albert Memmi in his article, "Caute, Fanon and Gesmar" opines that Fanon's work, particularly his concern with the black-white relation, reflects the attempt of a disappointed evoluè who was struggling to work out "the solution to his personal drama in political action and philosophy."[28] Irene Gendzier, in her book, *Frantz Fanon: A Critical Study*, objects to this interpretation insisting that, "the genius of the man (Fanon) lies in his ability to transcend the personal dimensions of that drama and to understand where it touched on human condition."[29]

Although Fanon's predicament and his situation were environmentally defined, the same cannot be said of is thought, his life and the man he made of himself. Hence, David Caute in his work, *Frantz Fanon*, argues that some distinctive personal quality and forces of temperament pulled Fanon back from the consequences of his own skill and environment. According to Caute, Fanon's method is to fuse the descriptive and normative, to put the "like it is" at the service of "like it ought to be."[30] This research demonstrates how both Fanon's struggle for his personal freedom and his concern for the liberation of his society are related in understanding Fanon's concept of freedom.

3.2 WHY AND HOW OF OPPRESSION AND URGENCY OF FANON'S REMEDY

Hussein Bulham in his work, *Frantz Fanon and the Psychology of Oppression*, asserts that Fanon's point that colonial economic substructure is also a superstructure, that the cause is also

---

[28] Albert Memmi, "Caute, Fanon and Gesmar," in *The New York Times Book Review (*March 14, 1971), 5.
[29] Irene Gendzier, *Frantz Fanon: A Critical Study* (New York: Random House, 1973), 4.
[30] David Caute, *Frantz Fanon(*New York: The Viking Press, 1970), 10-11.

the consequence, is yet to be adequately appreciated. According to him, "when Fanon focuses his discussion on oppressed blacks, he directed attention not so much to the why of oppression (as Hegel and Mannoni did) but to how the violence of oppression dehumanized all involved."[31]

This shift from the 'why' to the 'how' of oppression, for him, reflected Fanon's sense of urgency and search for the practical solution which neither Hegel nor Mannoni sought. What makes Bulham's assessment of Fanon particularly welcome is its double focus.

On the one hand, Bulham presents a meticulous and scholarly commentary in the familiar intellectual antecedents and affiliation of Fanon's work – Hegel, Marx, Freud, Adler, Jung, Tosquelles, Cesaire, Sartre – providing us in addition, with the most valuable account of Fanon's lesser known clinical writings composed during his politically decisive phase as a psychiatrist. At another level, Bulham intersects his political and intellectual biography of Fanon with the submerged history of the black diaspora as it has been inscribed in the racist, stereotypic discourses of Eurocentric anthropology and psychology, and as it has been institutionalized in the discriminatory, dehumanizing practices of the medical and psychiatric establishments. Thus, Hussein Bulham is important to understanding why there are some hasty conclusions in Fanon's.

3.3 UNCONSCIOUSNESS OF THE COLONIZED

Claudia Wright, in her article, "National Liberation, Consciousness, Freedom and Frantz Fanon", maintains that the colonized person according to Fanon was not a self-conscious person. The colonized person is a mystified person, one who alienated himself. The source of the alienation is the cultural impact of colonization, acceptance and adoption of a culture of the colonizer.[32] Hence, one of the results of colonial alienation is a colonial self-consciousness, a form of false self-consciousness. Colonial self-consciousness results in a fabricated inauthentic self. It is the artificial construction of the native or the colonizer, which has transformed the colonized into thing or object through the process of assimilation. Colonial alienation according to Claudia Wright includes an alienation from the authentic nation. Wright concludes that the issue of racism is an integral part of Fanon's analysis of colonialism as a social construct. The colonized is a creation of the colonizer. The project of freedom requires the decolonization of both categories of false consciousness, the white man and the Negro, the colonizer and the colonized.[33]

3.4 LIBERATED CONSCIOUSNESS

According to La Rose Parris, in "Frantz Fanon: Existentialist, Dialectician and Revolutionary," Fanon reveals the liberated consciousness of the colonized subject and the resultant liberated society as the pinnacle of psychoanalysis, dialectics, materialism and existentialism.

---

[31] Hussein Abdilahi Bulham, *Frantz Fanon and the Psychology of Oppression* (New York: Plenum Press, 1985), 120.

[32] Claudia Wright, "National Liberation, Consciousness, Freedom and Frantz Fanon," in *History of European Ideas*, vol. 15, nos. 1-3, (1996): 427 - 434.

[33] Claudia Wright,.431.

For her, Fanon accomplishes two unprecedented feats: Being and Freedom which seemingly reach apotheosis within the historical and political context of African diasporic liberation. Secondly, and somewhat paradoxically, European-centered schools of Western thoughts are used to posit the colonial subject: liberated consciousness as the quintessential site of existential actualization and the foundation for collective revolutionary action.[34] Fanon's position is that resistance to colonial oppression takes freedom out of the realm of abstraction and into the concrete, inequitable world of human relations. Hence, the inequalities of racism and colonial oppression can only be eradicated through a struggle for equality and freedom. This struggle begins with the individual's ontological and political awakening, the understanding that colonized subject must break the chains of mental enslavement. Consequently, there is an absolute necessity for a liberated consciousness in the creation of a liberated society. There is always a movement from self to the society in Fanon's dialectics of freedom.

3.5 BONDAGE AS AN IMPOSITION ON FREEDOM

Lewis Gordon, in *Fanon and the Decolonization Philosophy,* tries to unravel the meaning of dialectics of freedom. According to him, there is a dialectical movement, which follows thus: bondage is an imposition on freedom, on human being with the aim of creating non-human physical object—namely, animals that could obey complex commands. The reassertion of humanity of such beings is that call for liberation, which requires the co-ordination of freedom and liberty[35]. So, the dialectics becomes movement from the initial freedom to bondage imposed by colonialism and then, to liberation. The intermediate stage requires more than a curtailment of liberty since the goal of oppression is also to make the subject give up his or her freedom.

Another important observation that Gordon makes is that as a matter of praxis, decolonizing struggles and those against racial oppression do not begin on ethical but peculiarly political premises of constructing a genuine self–other relationship through which actual relations can become possible. According to Gordon, the dialectics of freedom becomes one from violence to politics and then to ethics. A more stable human environment is needed for ethical life, and this environment is only possible in a society where there is freedom.[36] The concept of decolonization is important to post-colonial studies of which this research belongs.

But the main focus of this research is how to move on from neo-colonialism to freedom.

---

[34] La Rose T. Parris, "Frantz Fanon: Existentialist, Dialectician, and Revolutionary," in *The Journal of Pan African Studies*, vol. 4, no. 7, (2011): 8.

[35] Lewis Gordon. "Knowledge and the Academy," in Elizabeth Hoppe and Tracey Nicholls 9.

[36] Lewis Gordon, "Knowledge and the Academy," in Elizabeth Hoppe and Tracey Nicholls,9.

3.6 INTERPRETATIONS OF FANON'S FREEDOM THROUGH HIS BIOGRAPHY

In his biography, *Frantz Fanon*, Peter Gesimar gives a detailed interpretation of the development of Fanon's ideas and beliefs.[37] However, there are some seemingly inconsistencies in Geismar's analysis. This is glaring in Geismar's inability to plunge into the hurly–burly of controversial and grand issues of race and racism, hostility and violence that burned within Fanon himself. In this way, Geismar overlooked the anguish that consumed Fanon and propelled his thoughts. He thus "leaves us with an abstracted portrait, with little attempt to evaluate, measure, criticize or interpret Fanon."[38]

However, Renate Zahar, in her *Frantz Fanon: Colonialism and Alienation*, evaluates Fanon's theory through the means of category of alienation and relates this to the growth of consciousness. She maintains that Fanon's argument is that the process of decolonization can be adequately interpreted only if the process of consciousness and the psychological mechanism produced by colonialism are taken into account. According to Zahar:

The colonized, by relaying the pressure of the colonial system under which he suffers and aiming it into his fellow sufferers, the colonized man acts against his own interest, that is to say, in an alienated manner, but if popular resistance is politicized and organized in such a way as to lead to acts of violence against the true enemy - the colonizer - the violence loses its criminal character.[39]

It is in this sense, as it shall be demonstrated later in Fanon's theory of freedom, that violence becomes emancipatory and a potential instrument of freedom.

On the other hand, Irene Gendzier evaluates the three biographies written on Fanon. She argues that David Caute has written brief and informative political biography. Renate Zahra has presented a Marxist critique of the concept of alienation in Fanon's work. And Peter Geismar produced a highly favourable biography replete with details not to be formed elsewhere. From these biographies, Irene Gendzier draws the conclusion that Fanon was concerned with the dynamics of acculturation as well as the effect this process had on the individual and the community. For Gendzier, Fanon recognizes that both the dominant and dominated were affected by this process of acculturation. This is the kind of the mutuality which was inherent in the discussion of human relations and communications in Hegel's master-servant paradigm and in Sartre's 'anti–Semite who created the Jew.'[40]

But Fanon's argument with Hegel in *Black Skin, White Masks* is that the pragmatic development of reciprocity that Hegel developed has to be remapped. This is the reason why Nigel Gibson, in his article, "Fanon and the Pitfall of Cultural Studies" suggests that "when the slave is black the development of recognition through labour is blocked off: the black is 'walled in' by colour."[41] In this therefore, he insists that Fanon offers another route, a dive into black consciousness. This

---

[37] Peter Gesimar, *Frantz Fanon* (New York: Dail Press, 1971).

[38] Iris Andreski., *Old Wives' Tales: Life Stories from Ibibioland* (London: Routledge and Kegan Paul, 1970), 190.

[39] Renate Zahar, *Frantz Fanon: Colonialism and Alienation* (New York: Monthly Review Press, 1974), 56.

[40] Irene Gendzier, *Frantz Fanon: A Critical Study* (New York: Random House, 1973), 50.

[41] Nigel Gibson. "Fanon and the Pitfall of Cultural Studies," in *Frantz Fanon : Critical Perspectives* edited by Anthony Allesandrini, 108.

move, according to Gibson provides an insight into Fanon's sharp critique of Sartre's collapsing race into a 'colorless class' and is developed in the *Wretched of the Earth* as the process of national consciousness. The point is not simply a reversal of Sartre's thesis of collapsing class into race. Rather than equate reciprocity with identity, Fanon grounds recognition in the moment of alterity and calls for recognition from the other while demanding that such recognition should not be a type that reduces the other to identity.

This dialectic of reciprocity, according to Gibson is therefore a result of the introduction of race, now made concrete in terms of national liberation movement, as not reducible to the dialectics of labour.[42] So, Fanon is not simply replacing one dialectics (that is, anti-colonial) with another dialectics (class struggle), but through a system of interpenetration, deepening each of the dialectics. The result is a much more open ended or, as Fanon would put it, 'untidy' dialectics, which can be best understood in the social context.[43]

Indeed, the various classifications and categorizations of Fanon by scholars are important in understanding how Fanon is relevant to modern political theories. For, the scholars' interpretations of Fanon capture the character of dialectics in Fanon's theory of freedom. Along this lane, these scholars attest to the fact that it is only through dialectics that a better appreciation of Fanon's theory of freedom could be achieved. As well, they largely agree that Fanon's ideas are better remedies for all forms of colonization of human freedom and political instability within nations.

---

[42] Nigel Gibson, Fanon and the Pitfall of Cultural Studies, 108.
[43] Nigel Gibson, 108.

CHAPTER FOUR

CLASSIFICATIONS AND APPROACHES TO FANON'S IDEAS ON FREEDOM

4.1 LIBERTARIAN AND EXISTENTIAL PHENOMENOLOGICAL INTERPRETATION OF FANON

In continuation, another important issue that scholars are concerned in relation to Fanon is how to classify or categorize or interpret Fanon. Basically, there are four competing, and in some instances mutually informing interpretations of Fanon, which include; the Libertarian interpretation of Fanon by Henry L. Galas Jnr., Gayatri Spivak, Homi, K Bhabha; the Marxist approach of Cedric Robinson; the Cultural Studies approach of Benita Derry, Abdul Jan Mohamed, Edward Said; and the Existential Phenomenological approach of Lewis Gordon[44]. According to Lewis Gordon, in his *Fanon: A Critical Reader,* studies in Fanon can be characterized into five stages[45]. The first stage includes the various application and reaction to his work. This stage is represented by revolutionary thinkers like Fidel Castro, Ché Guevera, Heuy Newton, Paulo Freire, reactionary texts of Hannah Arendt, Sidney Hook and the Marxist- Leninist Nguyen Wright and Jack Woddis.

The second stage primarily consists of biological texts best represented by Irene Gendzier, Peter Geismar, and David Caute. The third stage comprises of intensive research on Fanon's relevance on political theory. The works of Hussein Adam, Emmanuel Hansen and Renate Zahar are in this stage. The fourth stage, which is still underway, is linked to the ascent of postmodern cultural and post-colonial studies in the academy. This stage is represented by such scholars as Edward Said, Homi Bhabha, Abdul Jah Mohamed, Gayatris Spivak, Benita Parry and Henry Louis Gates Jnr. From the Marxist perspective, it is represented by Cedri Robinson. The final stage consists of engagements with the thoughts of Fanon for the development of original work across the entire sphere of human studies. Its purpose is neither to explore nor denigrate Fanon but instead to explore ways in which he is a useful thinker. Examples of works reflecting this

---

[44] Leonard Harris and Carolyn Johnson, "Forward" In *Fanon: A Critical Reader,* edited by Gordon, L. R. et al, (U.S.A: Blackwell Publishers, 1990),xvi.

[45] Leonard Harris and Carolyn Johnson, 5-6.

final stage is Hussein's *Fanon and The Psychology of Oppression* (1985), Tsenay Sereqeberhamn's *The Hermeneutics of African Philosophy*, Lewis Gordon's *Fanon and the Crisis of European Man*, Ato Sekyi Otu's *Fanon's Dialectic of Experience*.

Although Anthony Alessandrini, in *Frantz Fanon: Critical Perspectives*, has some reservations with this division he nevertheless, maintains that this version of the development of Fanon studies is a compelling one. According to Alessandrini:

While I would like to disagree with its explicitly teleological bent - the editors suggest that 'each stage represents an ongoing dialectical process' - what is particularly important about this account is that it forces us to re-think the assertion that Fanon's work has enjoyed resurgence in recent years.[46]

4.2 SUCCESSIVE STAGES AND DISTINCT FORMS OF FANONISM

Besides the previous classifications, David Caute further identifies three successive stages in the development of Fanon's theory of freedom[47]. The first stage is that of the alienated man (*Black Skin, White Masks*), second stage is that of the free citizens of Algeria (*Studies in a Dying Colonialism*) and the final stage is the socialist revolution (*Towards the African Revolution and The Wretched of the Earth*). He maintains that in Fanon's corpus, there is a movement from descriptive emphasis of phenomenology to the study of the dialectics of revolution. For him still, "Fanon was concerned with forceful overthrowing of the tyrannical order so that the colonized self might achieve freedom and authentic individuality in the process"[48] of this struggle.

Still on stages in Fanon's work, Reiland Rabaka, in his *Forms of Fanonism: A Critical Theory and the Dialectics of Decolonization,* maintains that in highlighting Fanon's unique solution to the problem of racism, sexism, colonialism, capitalism and humanism, five distinct forms of Fanonism have materialized. These distinct forms, according to Rabaka will enable people to explore ways in which Fanon is a useful thinker with regard to relieving the wretchedness of the wretched of the earth of the 21st century, and deconstructing and reconstructing African studies, racial politics and critical social theory in their anti-imperialist interests.[49] The forms of Fanonism, according to Rabaka are; Decolonialist Fanonism, Anti-racist Fanonism, Marxist Fanonism, Feminist Fanonism and Revolutionary Fanonism.[50]

Although there appears to be no clear lines between the forms, the study is wholly appropriate as Fanon is being analyzed in multi-dimensional levels. Of course, Rabaka is aware of this when he maintains that the dialectical attraction and repulsion in Fanon's studies can partly be attributed to the ambiguities inherent in Fanon's thought and mono-disciplinary anxieties

---

[46] Anthony Allesandrini, "Introduction: Fanon Studies, Cultural Studies, Cultural Politics" In *Frantz Fanon : Critical*

Perspectives, edited by Anthony Allesandrini (London: Routledge Press, 1999), 5.

[47] David Caute, *Frantz Fanon* (New York: The Viking Press, 1970),31.

[48] David Caute, 31-32.

[49] Reiland Rabaka, *Forms of Fanonism: Critical Theory and the Dialectics of Decolonization* (UK: Lexington Book, 2011),4.

[50] Reiland Rabaka, *Forms of Fanonism: Critical Theory and the Dialectics of Decolonization*, 4.

of many interpreters of Fanon's works. He concludes by saying that there should be a multi-disciplinary method and models of studies for interpreting Fanon.[51]

4.3 FANON'S IDEA OF FREEDOM AS SINGLE THEORETICAL CONSTRUCT

Jock McCulloch, in his *Black Soul, White Artifact: Fanon's Clinical Psychology and Social Theory*, records that Fanon's works form part of a single theoretical construct. This construct is both unified and essentially coherent even though the manner of Fanon's presentation of his theory is often fragmented and obscure. According to McCulloch, "there is no epistemological or methodological break between Fanon's earlier and later works."[52] In this regard, Ato –Sekyi, in his *Fanon's Dialectics of Experience*, agrees with McCulloch'S assertion that "we should read Fanon's texts as though they formed one dramatic dialectic narrative."[53]

4.4 BILATERAL APPROACH IN THE PURSUIT OF LIBERATION AND FREEDOM

In his further review of Fanon, Jock McCulloch argues that Fanon proposed bilateral approach in the pursuit of decolonization. The first aspect of this approach according to McCulloch involves the process of self-reflection. This process is similar to processes associated with psychotherapeutics. The second approach according to Jock however requires change in the spheres of education and popular culture. Indeed, Fanon for McCulloch initiates the existence of a further dimension suggesting a second path to liberation. This second path consists of a direct attack on the oppressive socio-economic conditions under which the African lives. According to McCulloch:

At times Fanon wishes to combine these two dialectics within a single struggle, while at others he separated them according to the geographies of Africa and the West Indies. Consequently, it is possible to interpret Fanon's concept of bilateral change, as recognition of the need for both psychological and economic renovation within each single colony, and as a designation of the differences between the African and West Indian environments.[54]

Indeed, Otu refers to this approach of Fanon as dialectics of experience.[55] Justifying this position, he states:

Dialectic because it narrates the generation of relation infinitely more complex than the mass relationship or simplifying logic of the colonizer-colonized opposition. Dialectics because it testifies to the dissolution of "two metaphysics"

---

[51] Reiland Rabaka, 297.

[52] Jock McCulloch, Black *Soul White Artifact: Fanon's Clinical Psychology and Social Theory* (New York: Cambridge University Press, 2002), 3.

[53] Otu Ato Sekyi, *Fanon's Dialectics of Experience* (London: Harvard University Press, 1996), 4.

[54] ·Jock McCulloch, *Black Soul White Artifact: Fanon's Clinical Psychology and Social Theory* (New York: Cambridge University Press, 2002), 77.

[55] Otu Ato Sekyi, *Fanon's Dialectics of Experience* (London: Harvard University Press,1996). 26.

of absolute difference to which colonizer and colonized alike subscribe. And dialectics because this movement of experience consists, according to Fanon, in a progressive enlightening of consciousness occasioned by the appearance or resuscitating of realities hidden from the inaugural purview of the colonial subject.[56]

---

[56] ·Otu Ato Sekyi, *Fanon's Dialectics of Experience*, 26.

CHAPTER FIVE

5.1 THE MEANING OF DIALECTICS OF FREEDOM IN FRANTZ FANON

Dialectics has to do with the movement of two opposing positions or ideas towards a better position or idea. Before Fanon, many philosophers, especially Hegel, Marx and Sartre, applied dialectics to explain the movement of history or human society towards freedom. Fanon has critically appropriated Hegel's allegory of Master and Slave in the Phenomenology in order to display the distinctive properties of the colonizer-colonized relation.[57] But there is more to Fanon's critical reading of Hegel's famous meta-political story. That story is after all, a signal moment in the affairs of the spirit, one paradigmatic form among the variegated "series of its own configurations", the series of shapes through which self-consciousness must journey in order to attain genuine knowledge, and of course, true freedom.

Thus, Fanon follows Hegel in describing the procession of the order of things and configurations of consciousness as a "pathway" to freedom. It is Fanon's interpretation of these movements, as demonstrated in his account of the relations between the colonizer and the colonized in the colonial situation that I refer as dialectics of freedom. The relation between colonizer and colonized is characterized by violence. The colonizer sees himself or herself as a master, who should be obeyed at all costs. And the colonized sees himself as a slave, who wants to take the position of the master. So, the relation between the colonizer and colonized is that of mutual suspicion as one guards the dividing line and the other fights to cross the dividing line of colonialism. Thus, in the colonial situation, the dialectics of space leads to the dialectics of freedom.

Moreover, Fanon's argument with Hegel in *Black Skin, White Masks* is that the paradigmatic development of reciprocity that Hegel developed has to be remapped. When the slave is black the development of recognition through labour is blocked off: the black is walled in by colour.[58] Fanon offers another route, a dive into black consciousness. This move provides an insight into Fanon's sharp critique of Sartre's collapsing of race into a colourless "class" and is redeveloped in "The

---

[57] Otu Ato Sekyi, *Fanon's Dialectic of Experience* (London, Harvard University Press, 1996), 25-26.

[58] Nigel Gibson, "Fanon and the Pitfalls of Cultural Studies," in *Frantz Fanon: Critical Perspectives*, edited by Anthony Allesandrini,(London, Routledge 1999),108.

Wretched of the Earth" as the process of national consciousness. Fanon was not simply trying to reverse Sartre's argument that class can be collapsed into race. Rather than equate reciprocity with identity, Fanon grounds mutual recognition in the movement or relation between selves, and calls for a recognition that reduces neither the self nor its other to identity. It is Fanon's examination of the relations and contradictions between the self and the other in the quest for freedom in the colonial situation that this research examines as dialectics of freedom.

Furthermore, Fanon's theory of freedom is dialectic because it narrates the contradictions and resolutions arising from the colonizer-colonized relations. These relations are between the thesis of colonialism and the antithesis of anti-colonial struggle, which would eventually be resolved in the synthesis of freedom with the attainment of real humanity by both the colonizer and the colonized. It is also dialectics because it testifies to the dissolution of the binary Manichean world of the white and black, beautiful and ugly, colonizer and colonized, and master and slave on which the colonial world is built on. It is also dialectics because this movement of freedom consists, according to Fanon, in a progressive enlightening of consciousness occasioned by the appearance or resuscitating of realities hidden from the inaugural purview of the colonized subject. [59]

Therefore, dialectics of freedom in Fanon is a school of thought forming "a single theoretical construct [60] or "one dramatic dialectical narrative."[61] It is a single theoretical construct used by Fanon to describe how the two opposing world of colonizer and colonized would be destroyed in order to give way to one world of the decolonized man, or the new man and to the new humanity.[62] In these, Fanon posits the restoration of true humanity through the freedom of the enslaved black man.

5.2 FEATURES OF DIALECTICS OF FREEDOM

A critical assessment of Fanon's theory of freedom shows some categorical terms, which are paired as contradictory yet necessary towards the delineation of the dialectics of freedom. These categorical terms are discussed as features of dialectics of freedom.

5.2.1 *Colonialism and Decolonisation*

The unquestioned and unverified prejudices of western anthropologists and historians had relegated the black man to the subhuman and irrational levels. This position was taken over by some reputable western philosophers who argued that the black man or the African lacked rational capacity. Hence, Immanuel Kant, in his work *Von Verschiedenen Rassender Menschen* published 775, held that the inferiority of the black race has biological character. Hegel on the other hand excludes Africa from what he considers the movement of history towards its fulfillment. These positions became a well-watered ground for justification of slavery and consequent colonisation

---

[59] Cf. Fanon Frantz, *Black Skin, White Masks*, 115-116; Fanon Frantz. *The Wretched of the Earth*, 31 &116.

[60] Jock McCulloch., *Black Soul White Artifact*, 3.

[61] [61] Otu Ato Sekyi, *Fanon's Dialectic of Experience* 4.

[62] Fanon Frantz, *Black Skin, White Masks*, 180-181

which Africans were taken as beasts of burden or savages that needed to be civilized. On this note, Hountondji observes that "Hegel provided a powerful philosophical base to the chorus of denigration of the non-white races which accompanied and buoyed up the European colonial white adventure all through the nineteenth and as well as into the twentieth century."[63]

Furthermore, the theory of French colonial rule, as reflected in the French colonial policies of assimilation and association, is based primarily on the revolutionary doctrine of the equality of all peoples and the assumption of the superiority of French culture and civilization, an assumption that as a corollary rest on the denial of the authenticity of indigenous culture. Frantz Fanon's experiences in Martinique and France pointed to the gap between theory and practice of assimilation. Although he had "assimilated" French values in Martinique, he discovered in Martinique and France that colonialist society was a rigidly stratified or racist society in which the colour question was an overriding one that precluded his admission to, and mobility within French society on equal socio-economic and political terms with white French men.[64]

It is because of Fanon's belief that colonialism has a philosophical foundation that he goes out to construct a strong anti-colonial philosophy that he believed could lead to the decolonization of the African. So, Fanon's dialectics of freedom is the anti- colonial philosophy.

In continuation, Fanon was not much concerned about the historical origins of modern colonial empires of Western Europe. Apart from some scattered references in the *Wretched of the Earth* and *Towards the African Revolution*, he ignored the question on why black Africa came under European control during the latter part of the nineteenth century. This omission demonstrates to a great extent, the contemporaneous focus of Fanon's writings on the one hand as well as his heavy reliance upon the traditional wisdom of Marxist theories of imperialism. Jack McCulloch argues that, "following in the footsteps of Lenin, Fanon believed that the colonisation of the third world was undertaken by the European states in order to advance their perceived economic interest."[65]

In the same vein, Fanon's critique of colonialism implies denial of the claim that colonialism was a modernizing factor. Fanon thus argues that colonialism had acted as a brake on the process of social change in pre-colonial Africa. Fanon has implicit notion of what life was in traditional or pre-colonial African societies. But he does not explain clearly what the nature of those societies was nor does he offer a paradigm of the pre-colonial African societies. This is the reason why Jinadu Adele suggested that it may be useful to look at Fanon's claim less as an anthropological or historical one but more as a logical reconstruction, which is then used as a yardstick for measuring the negative impact of colonial rule in African societies.[66]

Furthermore, according to Fanon, there are three distinct phases of colonialism: the extractive, the consumer and ultra-colonialism. During the initial phase, the extractive phase, Europe viewed the colonies primarily as a source of raw material. This phase led to the accumulation of capital that was to finance the most creative period of bourgeois capitalism. Later, the colonies became important as markets for European manufactured goods and investment. With consumer

---

[63] Paulin Hountondji, *African Philosophy, Myth and Reality* (London: Hutchinson University Library for Africa, 1983), 11-12.

[64] Jinadu Adele, *Fanon: In Search of the African Revolution* (Enugu: Fourth Dimension Publishers, 1980), 22.

[65] Jock McCulloch, 137.

[66] Jinadu Adele, *Fanon: In Search of the African Revolution*, 42.

colonialism, the role of national units in the domination of colonies gives way to zones of economic influence.

The end of this phase appears to parallel the dawn of imperialism without empires. And the third phase, that of ultra-colonialism coincides with the period of national independence. Fanon argues that since the economic equilibrium of the metropolis is dependent upon the maintenance of colonies, any genuine liberation movement would constitute a mortal danger to European imperialist interest.[67] Foreign domination, according to Fanon, brings about the colonial situation which is first of all a military conquest continued and reinforced by a civil and police administration.[68] Colonialism has created a Manichean society where there are two zones of the colonized and colonizer, native and settler, black and white. The zone where the natives live, according to Fanon, is not complementary to the zone inhabited by the settlers. The two zones are opposed, but not in the service of a higher unity. Obedient to the rules of pure Aristotelian logic, they both follow the principle of reciprocal exclusivity.[69] According to Anthony Allesandrini:

> the tension created in the two zones is a guiding principle in Fanon's narrative: on the one hand, is the Aristotelian logic with its mutually exclusive oppositions; and on the other hand, the Hegelian logic which stages the lack, the contradiction in the Arisotelian logic itself by introducing a subversive negation."[70]

Both Aristoltle's and Hegel's logics played out in *Fanon's Black Skin, White Masks*. The Aristotelian logic is exemplified by the master who only laughs at the consciousness of the slave. What the master wants of the slave is not recognition but work. Secondly, the Hegelian logic reminds both the master and the slave that the order of things is contingent and reversible. While the slave is always alert to the possibility of putting himself in the place of the colonizer, the master is compelled to guard the dividing line with caution. Fanon stages the breakdown of the Manichean structure by appealing to the colonized to "make history" and to start a "new history of man."

Moreover, the Aristotelian and the Hegelian systems of logic have a common denominator in the necessity of violence: in both cases, the master must be overthrown through violence. According to Fanon, colonialism is violence in its natural state and it will only yield when confronted with greater violence.[71] But, there is a fundamental difference between Aristotelian and Hegelian systems of logic. Anthony Allesandrini argues that the moment Fanon's theory of violence is based upon an Aristotelian logic, then Fanon will be trapped inside the scope of the double-bind and thus reproduce the Manichean logic. The violence will not upset its logic of substitution and the slave that yields to pure force will only be tomorrow's master. It is exactly

---

[67] Fanon Frantz, *Wretched of the Earth*, 51.

[68] Fanon Frantz, *Towards the African Revolution,* trans. Haakon Chevalier (New York: Grove Press, 1988), 81.

[69] Fanon Frantz, *Wretched of the Earth*, 30.

[70] Michael Azar, "In the name of Algeria: Frantz Fanon and the Algerian Revolution," in *Frantz Fanon: Critical* Perspectives, edited by Anthony Allesandrini (London and New York: Routledge, 1999),25.

[71] Fanon Frantz, *Wretched of the Earth*, 48.

here that Fanon finds his greatest challenge; how can Algeria replace France without reproducing its colonial structure?

Anthony Allesandrini's invocation of Hegel implies a fundamental promise in Fanon's thoughts in violence. In the "Preface" to the *Wretched of the Earth*, this promise finds its most hopeful expression, "to shoot down a European is to kill two birds with one stone, to destroy an oppressor and the man he oppresses at the same time: there remains a dead man and a free man". It is on the level of liberation and freedom that the fundamental difference between Aristotelian and Hegelian logic must be found. In the first case, liberation is primarily a question of transcending the dividing line, penetrating the other zone guided by its terrible watch dogs, and taking the colonizer's place.

In the other, the aim is to abolish the dehumanizing system of colonialism at its very roots, to liberate both the colonizer and the colonized. Fanon makes this point clearer when he said that an independent Algeria must not be "the result of one barbarism replacing another barbarism, of one crushing man replacing another crushing man. [72]

Jock McCulloch opines that Fanon, especially in *Black Skin, White Masks*, assumes that there are two dialectics governing the liberation of the Negro; the first is primarily economic and the second psycho-existential."[73] In terms of the analysis which Fanon presented in *Black Skin, White Masks*, these dialectics correspond roughly to the geographical and sociopolitical distance between the two continents of Africa and West Indies. Once the problem of economic alienation has been resolved, then the question of cultural liberation can be effectively posed.

Fanon's major dialectic in *Black Skin, White Masks* which was addressed to the psycho-existential alienation of the Negro is heavily derived from Sartre's *Ophee noir*, the thesis is white racism, the antithesis is negritude, or, alternatively the white mask, and the synthesis is a new humanism in a world freed from racism. The step from the second to the third term is bridged by Fanon's application of the psyche of ascent suggested by Casaire's subjective method. It is bridged by a process of self-reflection, which the progressive infrastructure of masks was intended to generate. Of course, this dialectic which is narrow is confined or specifically directed to the West Indian.

But the second dialectic applies to the condition of the African, who suffers directly from the crude economic exploitation: the thesis is white economic exploitation, the antithesis is social revolution, and the synthesis is a new social order. Although Sartre's dialectic implies that negritude must always lead the Negro beyond aesthetics to the threshold of socialist society, but Fanon's did not point to that conclusion. His actional man is not a socialist man. But Fanon was later to incorporate the two dialectics into the theory of revolutionary decolonization. Just as colonization is geared towards turning the African into a thing so is decolonization meant to restore the African back to humanity. According to Fanon, "decolonization is quite simply the replacing of a certain species of men by another species of men. Without any period of transition, there is a total, complete and absolute substitution."[74]

---

[72] Fanon Frantz, *A Dying Colonialism*, trans. Haakon Chevalier (New York: Grove Press, 1965), 32.

[73] Jock McCulloch, 54.

[74] Fanon Frantz, *Wretched of the Earth*, 27.

The proof that decolonization is successful is seen in the destruction of the colonial structure in its entirety. Hence, the necessity of decolonization is already evident, though in its crude state, in the lives and consciousness of the colonized. And the possibility of decolonization is equally experienced in the form of terrifying future in the consciousness of the colonizers. Thus, the dialectics comes about through the meeting of the thesis of colonization and the antithesis of decolonization and which brings out the synthesis of liberation. The dialectics of colonization and decolonization brings about a new creation; a liberated man. It changes both the colonizer and the colonized into new men. But Fanon maintains that decolonization is always violent. Although Fanon did not explain much on what decolonization entails but it could be ascertained from his argument that the end point of decolonization is liberation.

Liberation in this context, according to Gordon, is the movement from domination to freedom. It suggests a dialectical movement as follows: bondage is an imposition on freedom or human beings with the aim of creating non-human physical objects-namely, animals that could obey complex commands.[75] The reassertion of the humanity of such beings is their call for liberation, which requires the coordination of freedom and liberty. Thus, the dialectic becomes movements from freedom to bondage to liberation. Total liberation entails freedom, and the freedom which Fanon dialectically envisioned had double dimensions: it is at once socio-political and personal. With regard to the former, Fanon has in mind the freedom of the nation-state and/ or governmental apparatus. Concerning the later, he envisioned an existential freedom which refers to individual's consciousness of their freedom and of their free choice.[76]

5.2.2 Racism and Negritude

The most characteristic feature of colonialism is racism, which underpins ideologically the division of society into "human beings" and "natives" caused by the colonial process of production. According to Fanon:

> When you examine at close quarters the colonial context, it is evident that what parcels out the world is to begin with the fact of belonging to or not belonging to a given race, a given species. In the colonies the economic substructure is also a superstructure. The cause is also the consequence; you are rich because you are white, you are white because you are rich. That is why Marxist analysis should always be slightly stretched every time we have to do with the colonial problem.[77]

Negritude came as a result of the colonial racism. So, Fanon maintains: "It is the white man who creates the Negro. But it is the Negro who creates negritude."[78] Moreover, Jock McCulloch

---

[75] Lewis Gordon, "Fanon on Decolonizing knowledge," in *Fanon and the Decolonization of Philosophy*, edited by Elizabeth A. Hoppe and Tracey Nicholls (UK: Lexington Books, 2010),9.

[76] Reiland Rabaka, *Forms of Fanonism: Critical Theory and the Dialectics of Decolonization* (UK: Lexington Books, 2011),128.

[77] Fanon Frantz, *The Wretched of the Earth*, 30-31

[78] Fanon Frantz, *A Dying Colonialism*, 47.

traces the origins of Negritude to the black American Diaspora. According to him, the uniqueness of Negritude lay in the response of writers and poets to the subordinate and symbiotic relationship experienced by New World Blacks in all their contacts with whites.

The evolution of the literature and philosophy of Negritude can be traced from the Afro-Cuban renaissance movements of the early nineteenth century through the writings of E.W Blyden and Marcus Garvey to its concentration in the poetry and philosophy of Leon-Gontran Damas, and Aime Cesaire. Negritude was essentially a celebration of black African cultural values by blacks who had little or no first-hand knowledge of Africa.[79]

The quest for personal identity and the pursuit of abstract freedoms encouraged the growth of an ingrained ambivalence in the poetry, literature and social theory of negritude. Initially, there was ambivalence towards a collective past, which by being idealized became all the more remote. More so, there was ambivalence about the direction changes should take in order to accommodate traditional cultures. There was a tendency by some elite from the emerging states of Africa to hide under the cover of Negritude in order to avoid confronting the social and economic problems associated with the taking over power from the colonial masters. What the new elite saw in negritude was the opportunity to ignore all questions concerning the development of the productive forces and the distribution of wealth in favour of the civilization of an exotic nostalgia and personal advantage. It is to be noted that the first and still the most convincing attempt to come to terms with negritude as both an aesthetic and an historical force was made by Jean Paul Sartre in his famous essay *Orphee noir*, Sartre was an important influence in Fanon's intellectual development. More relevant still, Sartre's dialectical interpretation of negritude influenced all subsequent interpretations of Negritude. According to Sartre:

> In fact, negritude appears as the minor term of a dialectical progression: The theoretical and practical assertion of the supremacy of the white man is its thesis, the position of negritude as an antithesis is the moment of negativity. But this negative moment is insufficient by itself, and the Negroes who employ it know this very well; they know that it is intended to prepare the synthesis or realization of the human in a society without races. Thus negritude is the root of its own destruction; it is a transition and not a conclusion, a means and not an ultimate end.[80]

One of the most evident influences of *Orphee noir* in Fanon was seen in Fanon's typology of colonial literature. Fanon distinguishes between three phases of indigenous literary production. The first phase is the assimilationist literature, which is purely imitative and is geared to a metropolitan audience. This is followed by a period of "re-immersion" into the symbolism myths of indigenous culture. Although Fanon refrains from using the term, this obviously corresponds to the phase of negritude. And the final phase is the revolutionary period when national literature

---

[79] Jock McCulloch, 5.

[80] Cf. Jean Paul Sartre, "Ophee noir," in *Anthologie de la nouvelle poesienegre et malgache de langue Francaise* edited by L.S. Senghor (Paris: Presses Universitaires de France, 1969), xi, quoted in Fanon Frantz., *Black Skin, White Masks*, 102.

sets out to inform the people and awaken their political consciousness. It is true that "what begins as a fierce attack upon *Orphee noir* ends with Fanon's acquiescence to Sartre's dialectic.[81] Fanon makes no attempt to acknowledge this debt, and no reference to *Orphee noir* is made after *Black Skin, White Masks*, yet Fanon's changing attitude towards the negritude movement runs parallel with his gradual appropriation of Sartre's dialectic.

It was not until Fanon had accepted the dialectical significance of negritude that he could acknowledge the movement as politically and psychologically important. The progressive function of negritude consists of the negation of the colonial racism and the collection of one's own historical tradition, which colonialism threatened to consign to eternal oblivion. But even this negative revolutionary response to colonialism is deeply marked by what it rejects: it bears in itself racist features. The relativity of negritude stems from the fact that it has to rely on the methods of colonial ideology to react against it and even in the act of negating colonialism it reproduces its features. That is why Sartre rightly calls negritude "an anti-racist-racism".

Fanon criticized the established philosophy of negritude for trying to fabricate a black consciousness at a time when the colonial revolutions show that the "Negro" is ceasing to exist. According to Fanon, the writer's falling back on the past only has a meaning if it is linked in a concrete manner with present-day realities: otherwise its culture remains folklore.[82] But Fanon appreciates the importance of negritude to self-recognition and freedom of the blacks. Not only does it offer the black sources of pride, but the white suddenly recognizes in the Negro qualities such as closeness to nature, spontaneity, simplicity, which are lacking in western civilization.

Thus, for the first time, a certain reciprocity of recognition emerges. But the recognition, even if it is real, is ephemeral. For white culture still has at its disposal the overwhelming means of devaluing blacks' experience. Although Negro simplicity is said to be delightful, "History" is still on the side of rationalism, technology and industry which Europe represents. Negro culture thus becomes appropriated as a diversion, as a realm for momentary relaxation.

How can one transcend from negritude to freedom? Fanon answers by criticizing as irrelevant negritude's search for black identity through the retrieval of great African cultures of the past. Fanon also argues that resentment over past injuries and demands for reparations is misguided, for it represents an orientation towards the past whereas freedom is always oriented towards the future. Thus, "it is by going beyond the historical, instrumental hypothesis that I will initiate the cycle of my freedom."[83] Therefore, negritude helps the African to affirm his identity but this affirmation can only be liberating in the context of a struggle to transform the material and institutional forms of colonialism into praxis for decolonization.

5.2.3 *Motions of Language and Desire*

Fanon's main argument in *Black Skin, White Masks* is that the desire to be white wholly consumes the blacks. Fanon argues that some specific figures such as Mayotte Capecia and Jean

---

[81] Jock McCulloch, 53.

[82] Renate Zahar, *Frantz Fanon: Colonialism and Alienation* (New York: Monthly Review Press, 1974), 71.

[83] Fanon Frantz, *Black Skin, White Masks*,180.

Veneuse and more generally most non-whites living in the white culture desire ultimately to be white.

This may take the form of trying to control one's speech so as to pronounce "R's" in an acceptable fashion, taking on particular professions or marrying someone who is white. As obsessive neuroses, these acts bring them closer to being white and that is the main reason why they are carried out. A dominant reaction of the colonized subject is to refuse the binary essentialism of white and black which sustains the colonial order. The colonized tries to adapt to a world which reduces existence to an unchangeable essence and divides people according to racial membership and projects race as a foundation of subjectivity. Against the relentless racialization of the world, the racialized social group tries to imitate the oppressor and thereby to deracialize itself. The inferior race denies itself as a different race.[84]

The colonized people take the motion of language as a sign of a cultural conquest of difference and the motion of desire as a vehicle for establishing an affective community. By virtues of the motions of language and desire, the colonized institutionally "hemmed in", became a prisoner of an eternal essence, is reborn as a transcending subject who is sealed into a crushing object, and turns beseechingly into the world of the other, there to find an imagined community of meaning made flesh. Fanon portrays the acquisition of the master's speech as an emblematic rite of passage into the imagined transracial community. According to Fanon, "the Negro of the Antilles will be proportionately whiter, that is, he will come closer to being a real human being in direct ratio to his mastery of the French language."[85] So, the Negro believes that mastery of the colonizer's language will make him a real human being.

Equally, the colonized wants to be real human by desiring for the other dramatized in "the woman of colour and the white man" and "the man of colour and the white woman". The desire of the black woman to marry a white man and the desire of the black man to marry a white woman both point to the single project of the colonized to become whiter by engaging the white as the other. For Fanon, this desire for all its aggressive triumphalism is quite compatible with a constant effort on the part of the colonized to run away from his own individuality or to annihilate his own presence. Ultimately, neither the motion of desire nor the motion of language can undo the colonial context however fervently the colonized try to disown themselves. This is because no matter how seriously the colonized pursue the project of self-alienation; this alienation is never wholly successful.

When the colonized discovers that he cannot be white through the motions of language and desire, he experiences what Fanon calls a mutation in his or her consciousness. According to Fanon, "the futility of his alienation, his progressive deprivation, the inferiorized individual, after this phase of deculturation, of extraneousness, comes back to his original positions."[86]

Fanon sees the going back of the colonized to their original culture after the failed assimilation as dialectic. Thus, what is involved is not the emergence of ambivalence but rather a mutation, a radical change of valence, not a back-and-forth movement but a dialectical progression.[87] But

---

84 Otu Ato Sekyi, *Fanon's Dialectics of Experience* (London: Harvard University Press, 1996), 89.

85 Fanon Frantz, *Black Skin, White Masks*, 8

86 Fanon Frantz, *Towards the African Revolution*, 41.

87 Fanon Frantz, *A Dying Colonialism*, 90.

since the colonized cannot go back to his original culture again because the culture has already been compromised, what is needed to be done is a dialectical transcendence into the future.

5.2.4 The Self and the Other

The complexity of the challenge facing the colonized in the colonial situation is double-fold: that of facing an oppressive other and of overcoming the internalized and crystallized white attitude of viewing reality. In the first place, Gordon has argued that Fanon demonstrated the limit of the self-other dialectic in colonial situation. At the centre of this dialectic is the possibility of symmetry–the self that sees another as other is also seen by the other as its other.[88] There is a self/other–other/self-relation in which reciprocity beckons. But in the colonial situation, the relationship is one sided: it is one between colonizers or members of the dominating race. This is because according to Fanon, "at times, this Manicheanism goes to its logical conclusion and dehumanizes the native or, to speak plainly, it turns him into an animal."[89] Thus, the colonizer does not encounter another human being outside of himself: he encounters only "things".

On the other hand, the white civilization and European culture have forced an existential derivation on the colonized. This is because the colonized cannot live his own life rather his existence is derived from and dependent upon that of the European.

At this stage, the oppressive relation is no longer across white and black selves. It is internalized between black and white souls, among black and white selves and between black skin and white masks. W.E.B Du. Bois had earlier described the effect of the colonial situation on the colonized in a similar way, by maintaining that a Negro has "two souls, two thoughts, two unreconciled strivings and two warring ideas in one dark body.[90]

This experiencing of the multiplicity of selves with one another is also diagnosed psychoanalytically in terms of the neurons of the individual:

> the neurotic structure of an individual is simply the elaboration, the function, the eruption within the ego; of conflictual clusters arising in part out of the environment and in part out of the purely personal way in which the individual reacts to these influences.[91]

Furthermore, when it experiences these oppositions both within itself and outside of itself, the self is bound to experience some crises. According to Fanon, after all that has just been said, it will be understood that the first impulse of the black man is to say no to those who attempt to build a definition of him. It is understandable that the first action of the black man is a reaction. But this reaction is not enough and that is why Fanon criticized Negritude as not having the force to change the attitude of the colonized. Negritude succeeded in demonstrating the reaction of the

---

[88] Lewis Gordon, *Fanon on Decolonizing Knowledge*, 10.
[89] Fanon Frantz, *The Wretched of the Earth*, 32.
[90] W.E.B DuBois, *The Souls of Black Folk*, intro by S. Redding (New York: Dodd, Mead & Co, 1966),.3.
[91] Fanon Frantz, *Black Skin, White Masks*, 59.

black man to racial domination but could not propose line of action into changing the situation of the black man. But in the dialectic of self and other lies the liberation of the self.

According to Fanon, "there is a zone of non being, an extraordinarily sterile and arid region, an utterly naked declivity where an authentic upheaval can be born. In most cases, the black man lacks the advantage of being able to accomplish this descent into real hell.[92] It is here that one appreciates the importance of violence to freedom that Fanon so much talked about. It is through this descent to hell which is equivalent to doing some violence to oneself that one frees oneself from this colonial domination. Thus, personal freedom is assured through Fanon's application of the psyche of ascent as suggested by Cesaire's subjective method. It is a method of self-reflection.

The black man must confront the despair of his life's experience and thereby suffer the anguish of liberty. Fanon has never failed to demonstrate that freedom has two dimensions: personal and socio-political freedom. According to Fanon, he two dimensions of freedom are related since they depend and enforce each other. We agree with Fanon that "an authentic national liberation exists only to the precise degree to which the individual has irreversibly begun his own liberation.[93] Hence, a true liberation must involve a radical dissolution, not only, or even primarily, of the physical violence of the colonial situation, but ultimately dissolution of the inferiority complex and the alienation epidermalised in the colonized. It is this situation that choosing violence becomes choosing an existence that transcends mere life, to risk death for the foundation of a subjectivity and freedom of one's own.

5.2.5 Visibility and Invisibility

In a socio-political setting, there is always discursive opposition. Interaction in such a setting involves communicative possibilities that rely on the suspension of violent or repressive forces.[94] Fanon's corpus is concerned mainly with interrogating the interface of colonialism's various manifestations and resistance to them and thus overwhelming with the shifting and complex questions of "the color line". Whiteness has long been characterized in terms of light and learning and blackness in terms of darkness and degeneration. Thus, visibility carries with it connotations that tend to be appealing-access, opportunity, ability, in short, power and invisibility has tended to connote absence, lack, incapacity-in short, powerlessness. In the colonial situation, both the colonizer and colonized fight to be visible and invisible as the situation demands. The colonizer does not want the colonized to be visible at certain point in time but wants to be visible. But the colonized wants to be visible or invisible according to whether being visible or invisible ensures or obstructs his freedom as the case may be. It is Fanon's argument that through the struggle to be seen or unseen in the colonial situation that freedom is achieved and the colonial situation is destroyed. Hence, "man is human to the extent to which he tries to impose his existence on another in order to be recognized by him."[95]

Colonialism renders invisible the lines of power and controls both within the colony and

---

[92] Fanon Frantz, *Black Skin, White Masks*, 2.
[93] Fanon Frantz, *Towards the African Revolution*. 103.
[94] Lewis Gordon, 14.
[95] Fanon Frantz, *Black Skin*, 168.

especially-through the spatial and administrative technologies of distancing between absent colonizing power and people and their colonized counterparts. This sadistic invisibility makes possible the partial hiding from view of the source of characteristic control, domination, degradation, and oppression that is the mark of the colonial condition. Fanon maintains that "the colonized exerts a considerable effort to keep away from the colonial world, not to expose himself to any action of the conqueror."[96] Hidden from view, blind to the world and to themselves, the colonizers transform self-determining subjects into objects, and naturalized objects into colonial subjects and subjected peoples. But colonialism succeeds to the extent its social relations of power remain invisible, as long as their presumed naturalism goes unchallenged.

Goldberry argued that race extends visibility or invisibility to those it categorizes, and it may be used strategically to promote or deny recognition, social elevation and status. Whites assume visibility in virtue, though often in denial of their whiteness, and extend visibility to those upon whom whiteness lights. Recognized as blacks, black people at once are made visible in order to be rendered invisible. Fanon has argued that the logic offers only a cruel choice, only a deadly way out, and that is, into the white world: "Turn white or disappear". So the black people are forced with the dilemma that the principal mode of personal progress and self-elevation open to them is precisely through self-denial, effacement, and the obliteration of their blackness. The blacks are predicated upon the possibility of tendering a significant feature of their self-definition invisible, if not altogether effaced. This invisibility, in turn, is effected through the necessity of recognition by whites which is begrudgingly extended only at the cost of the invisibility of blackness.

The prevailing logic of whiteness is to make invisible the visible and visibly threatening. Fanon traces the dialectics of visibility and invisibility in the colonized use of the veil, radio and language. The veil serves in a complex way to maintain mystery, refuse mastery and hide history in a double edged resistant refusal. Seeing but not seen, the veiled woman is suggestive of the forbidden and impenetrable, a forbiddance and impenetrability that "frustrates the colonizer".

According to Fanon, "it was the colonialist's frenzy to unveil the Algerian woman, it was his gamble on winning the battle of the veil at whatever cost, that were to provoke the native's bristling resistance."[97] But Fanon was quick to observe that there is a historical dynamism of the veil that is very concretely perceptible in the development of colonization in Algeria. In the beginning, the veil was a mechanism of resistance, but its value for the social group remained very strong. The veil was worn because tradition demanded a rigid separation of the sexes, but also because the occupier was bent on unveiling Algeria. But in a second phase, the mutation occurred in connection with the revolution and under special circumstances. The veil was abandoned in the course of the revolution. So the veil became a means of making Algerian women invisible or visible to the colonizers as the circumstances demanded.

Furthermore, like the veil, the radio can be used to make visible from a place or position of relative invisibility, conditions of oppression and liberation. So, radio makes the invisible visible via explication, obviating, reporting and reviewing. Radio is also a means of revelation, or at least of concealing and revealing. As a technology, radio offers a medium for the dissemination

---

[96] Fanon Frantz, *A Dying Colonialism*, 130.
[97] Fanon Frantz, *A Dying Colonialism*, 46.

EVARISTUS EMEKA ISIFE

of information, but at once mediates the message. To inform is to give form to the empirical, to make visible the hidden and inaudible the spoken. According to Fanon, through the possession of radio, the truth of the oppressor so formerly rejected as an absolute lie, was now countered by another as acted truth. As the bearer of culture, language carries and conveys values, and these norms of conception and perception are often stereotype, and in stereotyping render invisible their objects of reference. The invisibility of stereotyping effects is produced by virtue of the fact that the person stereotyped emulates the anticipated reaction that the master's stereotype projects.

In the projection of white superiority and black inferiority, white visibility and black invisibility, the fragility of master -hood is reflected and refracted. As the presumptive norm of racial power and elevation, the racial dimension of whiteness could be denied, or at least ignored. If race is Other, whiteness is invisible and the site of racial power and arrogance. While whites could cower for so long behind the presumed invisibility of their whiteness, this paradoxically hides from view the very vulnerability of whiteness.

The presumptive invisibility of whites could be turned against them, their spoiled nature revealing fragility at the heart of whiteness, its decadence powerlessness possible to be challenged. Invisible in terms of its whiteness, white power is viciously visible in conception and effect but fragile in application and self-absorption. At such, whiteness can be confronted and condemned, resisted and restricted, diffused and defused.[98] Freedom comes in the dialectic of visibility and invisibility when the formerly invisible become visible while the formerly visible are frozen at the margins of their own fabrication, and thus become invisible.

5.2.6 Violence of the Colonizer and Counter Violence of the Colonized

The colonial situation is built on and sustained by violence. Fanon had earlier hoped that reason would prevail or that persuasion would change the oppressor-oppressed dialectic.[99] But the situation of things in Algeria proved him wrong. He then saw that only violence could transform the oppressive order and enslaved psyches built by the colonizers. The colonizer depended on and understood only violence and he had to be met with greater violence. According to Fanon, the violence of the colonial regime and the counter violence of the native balance each other and respond to each other in an extraordinary reciprocal homogeneity.[100] Thus, central to Fanon's theory is the notion that a Manichean psychology underlines human violence and oppression. A Manichean view is one that divides the world into compartments and people into different species. This division is based not on reciprocal affirmations, but rather on irreconcilable opposites cast into good versus evil, beautiful versus ugly, intelligent versus stupid, white versus black, human versus subhuman modes.[101] This duality is anti-dialectic and thus there is no attempt towards a higher synthesis. Oppression creates and requires such a psychology whereas at the same time violence too emerges from and reinforces the Manichean psychology.

Moreover, in this anti-dialectic Manichean colonial situation, it is only through the dialectic

---

[98] David Theo Goldberg, 199.
[99] Fanon Frantz, *Black Skin*, 5.
[100] Frantz Fanon, *The Wretched of the Earth*, 69.
[101] Hussein Abdilahi Bulham, *Frantz Fanon and the Psychology of Oppression* (New York: Plenum Press, 1985), 140.

32

of violence that freedom would be realized. According to Anna Carastathis, Fanon's conception of history is the basis for the normative necessity of violence in decolonization struggles.

This conception in turn, is grounded in Fanon's view of existential freedom. The dialectic progression towards freedom and authentic human existence must be initiated by the colonized subject. In more concrete political terms, this means that true decolonization cannot take the form of national independence conferred by the colonizing empire. Instead, the first moment in the progression must be an assertion of subjectivity on the part of the colonized people, which radically disrupts their systematic objectification, their dehumanization by the colonizer[102].

In the initial stage of decolonization, the primary Manicheanism, which governed colonial society and set an absolute division between settler and native is preserved. This is violence in action in the short term. But Fanon argues that revolutionary struggle also has a longer-term objective. It is also aimed at destroying the Manicheanism of the colonial situation. In so doing, it aims at destroying race. By destroying the settler, racial bifurcation of the colonial society is also destroyed. Thus, in Fanon, violence plays some important roles in the colonial situation. In the first place, since freedom of the black man begins from himself, Fanon proposes that violence has a cleansing force on the individuals.[103] It frees the individuals from his inferiority complex and from his despair and inaction and makes him fearless and restores his self-confidence.[104] Also, Fanon maintains that violence at the level of the society unifies the people. The people will have time to see that the liberation struggle has been the business of each and all and that the leader has no special merit from others.

Finally, one of the main critics of Fanon's theory of violence is Hannah Arendt. She accused Fanon of glorifying violence for violence's sake. Arendt not only placed Fanon in close affinity with Sorel and Paneto, as authors of rank, who glorified violence for violence's sake, but maintained that "Fanon, who had an infinitely greater intimacy with the practice of violence than either, was greatly influenced by Sorel and used his categories even when his own experience spoke clearly against them."[105]

But Fanon's goal to heal tormented psyches moved from the consulting room to the larger societal arena, from a concern with private and personal problem to an emphasis on public and collective well-being, and from curative and institution –based to preventive and mass participatory measures. For Fanon, violence is never an end in itself but only a last recourse - and a perilous one for that.[106] So, violence is only a means not the end of freedom. And when freedom is realized, there will be no need for violence.

---

[102] Anna Carastathis, "Fanon on Turtle Island: Revisiting the Question of Violence," 86.

[103] Fanon Frantz, Black Skin, 2.

[104] Fanon Frantz, *The Wretched of the Earth*, 74.

[105] Hannah Arendt, *On Violence* (New York: Harcourt, Brace & World, 1970), 71.

[106] Hussein Abdilahi Bulham, *Frantz Fanon and the Psychology of Oppression*, 146.

CHAPTER SIX

ANTITHESIS OF VIOLENCE IN THE DECOLONIZATION OF THE OPPRESSED

6.1 ON THE ROLE OF REVOLUTIONARY VIOLENCE

On the role of violence in Fanon's dialectics of freedom, Gendzier argues that for Fanon, violence was indispensable to the process of decolonization but it was inadequate to it, and it was not raised to the state of a permanent policy either in the decolonization process or after.[107] It was for this that Jinadu Adele, in his article, "Review of Frantz Fanon: A Critical Study by Irene Gendzier", argues that there is a major weakness in the discussion on violence by many scholars which is the failure to distinguish between Fanon's thesis that the colonial situation is an inherently violent one and his ethical justification of violence as a potent instrument of liberation.[108] Adele gives Gendzier the credit for avoiding the one-sided treatment of the role of violence in Fanon by placing the topic in the wider perspective of colonial violence. Adele points out the weakness in Fanon's thesis that true liberation is achieved only when one fights for it: while false liberation occurs or obtains where freedom is granted or conceded by the alien power.

According to Adele, it does not necessarily follow from the fact that if freedom is granted to a slave for example, that the slave will not appreciate the value of his or her newly-acquired freedom or work hard to preserve it. While there may be some basis for the claim that to be indebted is to compromise one's freedom to act, the claim is by no means self-evident. Adele, in his work, *Fanon: In Search of the African Revolution*, maintains:

> Fanon's mistake is in confusing two different issues. It is one thing to state a preference for struggling to free oneself. It is another thing to claim that where freedom is achieved without struggles people will not appreciate it or will eventually compromise their newly-won freedom. [109]

---

[107] Irene Gendzier, *Frantz Fanon: A Critical Study* (New York: Random House, 1973), 50.

[108] Jinadu Adele, "Review of Frantz Fanon : A Critical Study by Irene Gendzier," in *The Journal of Developing Areas* vol. 8, no. 2, (1974):300 – 03.

[109] Jinadu Adele, *Fanon: In Search of the African Revolution* (Enugu: Fourth Dimension Publishers,1980), 82.

By way of continuation, Adele, in his article, "Some Aspects of the Political Philosophy of Frantz Fanon", questions what Fanon means by a "true decolonisation". As far as the relationship between means and ends is concerned, the question of whether a particular means (strategy) by itself ensures a particular result- Fanon appears to be undecided.

According to Adele, "in a passage in the *Wretched of the Earth* that is often overlooked, Fanon concedes that a strategy short of violence may be appropriate in certain cases."[110] The issue is that if Fanon was aware that the strategy of the decolonization was dictated by situation, it would be hard to understand his blunt assertion that "violence alone, violence committed by the people, violence organized and educated by its elders, makes it possible for the masses to understand social truth, and gives them key to them."[111] Adele concludes by stating that any rebellion whether violent or nonviolent is a leap in the dark and success or failure of a strategy becomes an issue after not before it is used, which is contrary to Fanon's impression that success was inevitable in the case of resort to violence in Algeria.[112]

In the same note, Anna Carastathis, in her article, "Fanon on Turtle Island: Revisiting the Question of Violence", maintains that freedom for the colonized is bound up with violence. According to Anna Carastathis, violence is found not only in the Manichean division between settlers and colonized in the colonial situation but also "violence is the means through which the colonized find their freedom."[113] This emancipatory violence for Carastathis reciprocates the violence of colonial rule. Violence constitutes the negative moment of decolonization, which is necessary for the decolonization of the colonized, and by extension of the colonizer.

But Mohammad Tamdgidi was quick to point out that to detach Fanon's argument about the role of violence in the dialectics of freedom for a cruder form of revolutionary violence pertaining to a particular stage of colonial domination, and to advocate that for all anti-colonial struggles including those in the present period, the neo-colonial period, when the modes of domination are mediated through the machinery of a capitalist enterprise firmly established in the former colonies, would be an exercise in ahistorical analysis.[114]

And Robert Bernasconi in his article, "Casting the Slough: Fanon's Humanism for a new Humanity", maintains that violence has a different result depending upon who does it and who suffers it. It is only the violence of the colonized against the colonizer that is positive. Whereas the colonizers are committed to keeping the oppositional relation intact, the violence of the colonized is dialectically transforming both colonizer and colonized into a new humanity.[115] It is in the fighting for liberation that the liberation struggle is dialectical. It is the dialectical development

---

[110] Jinadu Adele, "Some Aspects of the Political Philosophy of Frantz Fanon," in *African Studies Review*, vol.16, no.2, (1973):246.

[111] Jinadu Adele, Some Aspects of the Political Philosophy of Frantz Fanon,246

[112] Jinadu Adele, Some Aspects of the Political Philosophy of Frantz Fanon, 265.

[113] Anna Carastathis, "Fanon on Turtle Island: Revisiting the Question of Violence, 87.

[114] Muhamed Tamdgidi, "Decolonizing Selves: The Subtler Violence of Colonialism and Racism in Fanon, Said and Anzaldua," in Elizabeth A. Hoppe and Tracey Nicholls, 123.

[115] Robert Bernasconi, "Casting the Slough: Fanon's New Humanism for a New Humanity," in L.R. Gordon et al, 119.

where something that was viewed as part of colonial system of oppression is taken over by the colonized and used by them in the struggle.

In the same note, Lewis Gordon sees the colonial situation as a tragic situation. For him, "the tragic lesson is that setting things 'right' and thereby setting the community right, calls for violent intervention–horrible intervention. He maintains that tragedy addresses the terror of mediation in the colonial context.[116] The role of violence in Fanon remains contentious and delicate as scholars try to interpret and apply violence in the post–colonial studies.

6.2 NECESSITY OF VIOLENCE

With his own argument, Ferit Gúven maintains that Hegel's master- slave dialectic cannot work in the context of the relationship between the white and black slave mainly because of the conflict and struggle involved in the colonial context. The general appeal to the necessity of struggle seems to configure Fanon's later insistence that violence is necessary for decolonisation.[117] But Fanon's concept of struggle in *Black Skin, White Masks* as the argument goes, does not resist the Hegelian dialectics, but rather affirm its operation. However, when Fanon conceptualizes the idea of violence in the *Wretched of the Earth*, he is much more conscious of the necessity of interrupting the Hegelian dialectic in the colonial context.

Therefore, Fanon appeals to the necessity of violence in order to interrupt the violence of colonialism or rather neo-colonialism. It would be a mistake to interpret Fanon as condoning violence in a straight forward way. This is because Fanon sees violence as an existential interruption of Hegelian dialectic in the colonial context. So, what needs to be interrupted, and this is precisely what Fanon implies by violence, is the movement of Hegelian dialectics, which moves colonialism into a new form of neo-colonialism through sublation.

Hence, the conceptual interruption of Hegelian dialectics is vital for the process of decolonization.[118] It is a truism that colonialism has moved to neo-colonialism in most African countries. Hence, the role violence played in the colonial period is understood in this discourse to be relevant in present neo-colonial African epoch.

---

[116] Lewis Gordon, "Fanon's Tragic Revolutionary Violence." 298.

[117] Ferit Guven, "Hegel, Fanon and the Problem of Negativity in Post-Colonial," in Elizabeth Hoppe and Tracey Nicholls, 167.

[118] Ferit Guven, "Hegel, Fanon and the Problem of Negativity in Post-Colonial," 178.

CHAPTER SEVEN

NIGERIA AS A GEO-POLITICAL ENTITY

7.1 PRIOR TO NIGERIA AS A GEO -POLITICAL ENTITY

The geo-political entity known today as Nigeria dates from 1914 amalgamation of two British protectorates of Northern and Southern Nigeria by Lord Fredrick Lugard.[119] Prior to the amalgamation, what is known today as Nigeria comprised of disparate and independent traditional geo–political territories inhabited by different peoples. These peoples were pursuing their different destinies at their chosen pace. And many decades before the advent of the white man, each of these different peoples had attained some varying level of civilization. This was such that what the European colonialists encountered on their arrival were mainly already existing and organized ethnic nationalities. These nationalities included the highly politically structured group in the West–the Yoruba, a blend of the Hausa and Muslim Fulani in the North, and a configuration of decentralized republican clans held together by the common bond of language and culture–the Igbo in the East.

Also found in existence by the colonialists were vast numbers of other smaller tribes. These tribes, though variously associated with the major political and quasi–political entities, still preserved their independence and pursued their progress each in a distinctive manner. Hence, from the time of the creation of Nigeria in 1914 to the eve of the Independence on October 1, 1960, the colonial masters ruled these fragmented tribes or ethnic nationalities as an entity. It can be stated without any equivocation that "political instability in Nigeria began from the 1914 coercive amalgamation of diverse ethnic groups into one entity."[120] Therefore, in post-independence period, political instability has plagued the entire Nigerian polity. This is such that it has become a canker worm eating deep into the fabrics of socio-political and economic development of Nigeria.

---

[119] Lord Frederick Lugard was the first Governor-General of Nigeria. He was the man that carried out the unification of Northern and Southern Nigeria into one political entity now referred to as Nigeria.

[120] Evaristus Emeka Isife, "Political Instability in Nigeria: Causes, Impacts and Philosophic Solutions,".in *AMAMIHE: Journal of Applied Philosophy*, vol. 18, no. 6,(2020): 2.

7.2 SOCIO-CULTURAL DISTINCTIVENESS AMONG NIGERIAN ETHNIC NATIONS

It is worth noting that inherent in the distinctiveness that characterizes Nigeria's nationalities are certain internal socio-cultural variations that imparted on political development of these nationalities before colonial conquest, during colonial rule, and which have continued to impact on the political development in Nigeria since independence.

These variations could be understood in the light of Harry Eckstein's congruence theory. According to this theory, the political (in) stability in a polity is a function of the degree to which the authority patterns of its governmental and segmental units are congruent with one another and consonant within themselves.[121]

Apart from the Hausa-Fulani, the Igbo, Yoruba, and almost all the other nationalities that inhabit the Niger basin had evolved deeply democratic authority patterns across time before colonial conquest. Devoid of all the democratic traits that characterize the authority patterns by other nationalities that inhabit the Niger basin, society in post Jihad Hausa land and the rest of the areas that came under the control of the Fulani-dominated Sokoto Caliphate Empire functioned on the basis of an entrenched autocratic authority pattern in which submissiveness was the norm.

Thus, when Frederick Lugard was assigned to spear-head the conquest and imposition of classical colonial rule in the upper Niger, he was quick to notice the autocratic characteristics of the Hausa-Fulani authority patterns right after he had routed their forces in the plains of the city of Sokoto in 1904. As the first high commissioner of the Protectorate Government of Northern Nigeria, Lugard adopted the Hausa-Fulani rulers as allies and co-opted their autocratic authority patterns into the equally autocratic regime that he had already cultivated in the protectorate.[122] On the other hand, Lugard's counterparts who were assigned to accomplish similar task in the lower Niger wasted no time to dismantle crown colony rule in the Yoruba Kingdom of Lagos where returnee ex-slaves, their descendants, and indigenes who emulated them and embraced western education, culture and new commerce, formed a vital bridgehead for the projection of British authority in a manner that proved consonant and congruent with Yoruba authority patterns.

Along this line, Ejiogu marshals out four main policies formulated and implemented by Britain to preserve and extend Hausa-Fulani authority patterns to the rest of the nationalities that make-up Nigeria. These policies include the Indirect Rule, colonial education policy, policy for the recruitment of indigenous men into the military and the amalgamation policy of 1914.[123]

Apart from the fact that these policies ensured the preservation and extension of the Hausa-Fulani authority patterns to the rest of the nationalities, it was also at the root of mutual suspicion between the North and South on the wake of Nigerian Independence and up till the first six years of the civilian administration. This mutual suspicion later dovetailed into the 30 months civil war

---

[121] Harry Eckstein, "Authority Patterns: A Structural Basis for Political Inquiry," in *The American Political Science Review,* vol. 67, no. 4,(1973):1142-61.

[122] E.C Ejiogu, "The Roots of Political Instability in Nigeria,"1 -21, accessed September 14, 2021 from https: // wwwdocs.hsrc. ac. za. Ejiogu-the-roots-of-political-instability-in-nigeria.

[123] E.C Ejiogu, "The Roots of Political Instability in Nigeria".

and ensured that the Nigerian military stayed long in power. Apart from the 1963 constitution, which was stopped by the military, there was no serious attempt to restructure Nigeria along authority patterns that will be congruent with the understanding of politics and governance among Nigerian ethnic nationalities.

CHAPTER EIGHT

POLITICAL INSTABILITY AND ITS CONSEQUENCES ON THE NIGERIAN MASSES

8.1 CONFLICTING POLITICAL INTERPRETATIONS AND IMPLEMENTATIONS

Political instability in Nigeria consists in conflicting "interpretations, understandings and applications of political doctrines imbibed from diverse cultural backgrounds"[124]. In this way, the political managements involved often create antagonistic tempos that foul political stability. This stability is truncated further by political gestures from individuals within the management as each try to actualize his political and cultural demands or expectations. These conflicting actions of those in government are often exacerbated by the forces of greed and poverty which cause all kinds of dysfunctions in people.

8.2 RENEGING OF SOCIAL CONTRACTS

The act of reneging of social contract is political instability in itself. This is a conscious neglect of the reasons for leadership or the terms upon which leaders are elected. These terms include the provision of good life for all citizens, protection of life and properties, promotion of common good and interest. Negligence of these terms amount to breaching of social contract between the people and leaders and signifies political instability. The social contract is made on every election at the polls. And more instability emerges as reneging the social contract propels the people to disobey laws which they are only bound and obligated to obey once the social contract is kept. Odoziobodo explains this better when he submits that:

the logic of the social contract theory dictates that in so far as the people have entered into a contract with their government they are under the obligation to obey laws; then the government

---

[124] Evaristus Emeka Isife. "Political Instability in Nigeria: Causes, Impacts and Philosophic Solutions," 4.

agrees to protect and provide goods and services to the people who in turn render their obedience to the laws of the state.[125]

This kind of social contract is reciprocal between the state and the citizens.[126]

8.3 PRESSURE FROM THE MASSES AND CIVIL SOCIETY ORGANIZATIONS

The pressure of the masses and civil society organizations are evident in large upheavals; demonstrations, riots, agitations and industrial actions or strikes that thwart political processes and redirect governance. This form of political instability is consciously carried out and it is called civil disobedience.[127] Indeed, this pressure makes decision making and implementation in the corridor of government to wobble. In other words, expression of grievances or displeasure with governance from the masses amounts to political instability. This becomes more pronounced as such condition attacks the legitimacy of leaders, rightness of their actions and deprives them of the confidence of the people. With this confidence punctured, the government becomes unpopular and this affects the stable trend of governance.

8.4 POLITICAL MANIPULATIONS

Political manipulation is a kind of cutting corner to achieve political objectives. It truncates stable politics and governance, and remains an evident political instability. Political manipulation is more evident in political lobbying, maneuvering, coercion, manipulation of electoral processes, imposition of political candidates on the people, etc. Thus, as pertains to Nigerian polity, Akubue describes it further as:

> ...stocking of arms and schooling of hapless youths on how to intimidate, maim and kill those who may dare to challenge their bizarre ambition as a political rival. Arms are being stocked and thugs trained as part of preparation for the election days. We also have bribery. The politicians devise all sort of avenue of bribing the populace. In this, people's choice and conscience are bought over often with insignificant gains. ...Elections in Nigeria are war, dissension and assassination. Elections in Nigeria are simply a subversion of democracy and political mistrust and democratic sycophancy.[128]

---

[125] Severus Ifeanyi, Odoziobodo, *Society & Revolution: A Nigerian Perspective* (Enugu: Education Promotion Agency, 2003), 15- 16.

[126] See also, Jean-Jacques, Rousseau, *The Social Contract*, trans. Maurice Cranson (England: Penguin Books, 1968), 59-63.

[127] Severus Ifeanyi, Odoziobodo, *Society & Revolution: A Nigerian Perspective*, 20-38.

[128] Tochukwu Daniel Akubue, *Fulfilled Dreams of Martin Lurther King Jnr: A Challenge to Nigerian Democracy* (Enugu: Ndubest Productions, 2010), 34-35.

In short, it is just summarized as "political charade."[129]

8.5 IRRESPONSIBILITY AND IRRESPONSIVENESS

This is another tangible cause of political instability in Nigeria. It is evident in government apathy towards the suffering, opinion and cry of the people. Irresponsibility in this context therefore means government action being contrary to rule of law, principles of governances, dictates of human conscience and human responsibility.[130]

Thus, the several negligence of duty within the context of politics and governance is political instability. Along this line, the inability of government to respond to issues as well as its lackadaisical attitude towards issues of national importance amounts to political instability.

8.6 POLITICAL DESPOTISM AND TYRANNY

Based on its criminality and predatory nature, political despotism truncates the trends and processes of governance. It weakens every opposition that would have brought dialectics with fruitful synthesis within the polity. It again robs the masses and neglects fruitful policies and incentives that benefit the masses. Despotism and tyranny make every political setting direly unstable as the despot and his cronies aim at that which satisfies their egoistic aggrandizement. In this way, Nigerian leaders betray every hope and legacies and leave the polity with political instability.

8.7 SYSTEMIC CORRUTPTION

Systemic corruption is "a situation in which corruption becomes an integrated aspect of the economic, social and political system such that honesty becomes irrational."[131] Systemic corruption is opposed to sporadic corruption which is petty and incidental in the political process. Systemic corruption therefore becomes political instability as it direly impacts on sustainable development. In other words, it shortens individual and government income and liquidates treasury leading to neglect of infrastructural development and provision of good life for the citizenry.

8.8 CONSEQUENCES OF POLITICAL INSTABILITY ON NIGERIAN MASSES

In this inherited political structure, a heritage that has "made post-independence Nigeria a continuation of colonial governance"[132], made with its incessant political instability, political

---

[129] John Odey, *This Madness Called Election 2003* (Enugu: Snaap Press Ltd., 2003),back page.

[130] See James Hojo, *Nigerian Government and the Youth, What is Happening?* (Orlu: Ogechi Press, 2009), 5.

[131] See Stanley C. Igwe, *How Africa Underdeveloped Africa* (Port Harcourt: Prime Print Technologies, 2012), 84.

[132] Evaristus Emeka Isife, Political Instability in Nigeria : Causes, Impacts and Philosophic Solutions, 4.

stability is impeded and the Nigerian masses are at the dire receiving end. Openly, the political class and elites while maintaining the poor Nigerian political *status quo* exploit these masses for their selfish ends. As such, the masses which comprise of the larger population are consistently pushed to the fringe of existence. Also at the middle of political instability in Nigeria is absence of universal recognition which is the fundamental human longing, the fulcrum of liberal democracy and civil society.[133]

The resultant effect of this is state of anarchy with increasing devaluation of human life and extra-judicial killings of the poor masses. In fact, Nigerian state is at the peak of Trasymachus' "might is right" and "justice being the interest of the stronger."[134] Amidst these, are deprivation of social justice and conducive atmosphere necessary for economic activities to thrive. As such, poverty and corruption are soaring high in every sector of the country breeding all kinds of dysfunction in the larger population. For instance, it is stirring the deep rooted need in humans which bothers on feeling at home in this universe.[135]

From this irrational urge and need therefore springs all kinds of crime which are becoming endemic in Nigeria. Coupled with these, Emeka Chinweuba contends that:

> the common citizens face the challenges of being exploited, intentionally delayed or ignored by security institutions in their quest for security rights, legal institutions in their quest for justice, educational institutions in their quest for knowledge financial institutions in their request for funding, communication institutions in their efforts to bring their goods and services to the public and other public institutions in their efforts to access necessary services needed for socio-economic development. Worst still, the citizenry face the threat of their output being unjustly taxed or expropriated by Politicians and their cabals in government when they resist compliance. These are exacerbated by unlawful arrests, security and law enforcers' intimidations of the public and especially the business rivals of the Politicians. Consequently, Emeka Chimweuba maintains that initiatives, talents, ambitions, investment, inventions, innovations and long term productivity of the greater population of Nigerians are generally hindered.[136]

Because incessant political instability has affected production, industry, agriculture and services, there has been unabated economic recession, absence of job opportunities and unemployment. These are aggravated by increasing taxation, tariffs, rates and bills to raise income for government.

These poor conditions have indeed affected the rational functioning of the psyche of greater Nigerians. As such, the greater Nigerian population is now deprived of critical therapeutic and

---

[133] Francis Fukuyama, *The End of History and the Last Man* (New York: Penguin Books, 1992), 288.

[134] Enoch Samuel, Stumpf. *Philosophy History & Problems.*(New York: McGraw-Hill, 1994), 33-34.

[135] Edwin Arthur Burtt, *Religion in an Age of Sciences* (London: William and Norgate, 1970).

[136] Gregory Emeka, Chinweuba, "Politics: The Dialectical Base of Poverty and Prosperity in Nigeria," in *Nnamdi Azikiwe Journal of Philosophy,* vol. 11, no. 2, (2019): 39.

renovative act as well as right judgment that ought to occupy the mind in order to purge it of inferiority, pessimism and oppression.[137]

Consequently, the worst of characters in the corridor of Nigerian politics that are ready to offer money have no short supply of army of supporters from the poor and downtrodden masses. Based on this, political instability in Nigeria has rendered many as veritable cannon fodders for escalating restiveness existent in the country.[138]

With many of the masses frustrated, some are indifferent to the situation because it has overwhelmed them. Some of the masses have resorted to violent agitations in order to register their displeasure with the ugly scenario. Therefore, just like the masses in Frantz Fanon's theory initiated the revolutionary process, so the Nigeria's masses are expected to initiate the revolutionary process to freedom. In all these, the actions of the elite and the reaction, and in some cases, the inactions of the masses threaten the corporate existence of Nigeria. But since Nigerian political elites lack the political will to move away from the colonial structure, the onus as submitted by Fanon still lie on the masses to regain their freedom. Thus, the masses must be inspired and encouraged, or if possible compelled, to initiate the movement towards decolonization, liberation and freedom.

---

[137] Ogbu Kalu, "Tradition in Revolutionary Change," in Ikenga *Journal of African Studies*, vol. 3, nos. 1 & 2,(1975): 55.

[138] Cf. John Nwodo, Restructuring *Nigeria: Decentralization for Normal Cohesion*. Chatham House: The Royal Institute of International Affairs, 27 September, 2017, 1; Gregory Emeka, Chinweuba. "Restructuring Nigeria: A Critical Study of its Relevance in Sustainable Development," in Sapientia *Journal of Philosophy*,vol. 10 (2019): 143.

CHAPTER NINE

FOUNDATION AND CAUSES OF POLITICAL INSTABILITY IN NIGERIAN STATE

9.1 POOR POLITICAL DEVELOPMENTS AND GOVERNANCE

The history of political development and governance in Nigerian state can be described as the biblical alegory of a "house built on soil." The foundation was bound to fall or fail because it was faulty and unstable.

9.1.1 *First Nigerian Republic*

The colonial epoch was replete with nationalists who were products of colonialism and collaborators of erstwhile colonists. These nationalists devoted much energy to taking power and control of Nigerian affairs from the British colonists. Rather than working out progressive policies for the emerging Nigerian nation, most of these nationalists acted as indigenous colonists. Reports of the Constitution Drafting Committee (CDC) reiterates this reality in its criticism of First Republic politicians (nationalists) observing that their preoccupation with power and material benefits deprived their minds of political ideologies as to how a society can be organized and ruled to the advantage of all.[139] Nwafor Orizu also reiterates this poor foundation by submitting that:

> the next six years until the achievement of independence on 1st October, 1960, Nigerian leaders were preoccupied so much with wrestling power from the colonial government rather than on deciding with day to day administration and development of the country as well as settling the basis on which they would cooperate with each other.[140]

With 1954 constitution, Nigeria was set for independence from Britain. But because required

---

[139] *Reports of the Constitutional Drafting Committee 1*(Enugu: Ministry of Education and Information, 1979), 35.
[140] Nwafor Orizu, *Without Bitterness: West Nations in Post War Africa* (Enugu: Nwaife Publishers Ltd, 1981), 236.

progressive and stable change was not focused on, political instability rooted in colonial structure continued after Nigeria's independence.

Prior to independence, three political parties participated in preparatory election held in 1959. These parties were the National Council of Nigeria and Cameroons (NCNC), which controlled the Eastern Region, dominated by the Igbo and led by Nnamdi Azikiwe; the Northern People's Congress (NPC) which controlled the Northern Region, dominated by the Hausa and Fulani and led by Ahmadu Bello and the Action Group that controlled the Western region, dominated by the Yoruba and led by Obafemi Awolowo.

With political parties formed along ethnic and tribal lines, Nigeria was charged with tribal politics and political instability. At a broader level, party politics took on the identity and ideology of each of the three main regions; the North, West and East. For instance, the Northern People's Congress (NPC) came with the motto; "One North, One People". As such, NPC resisted the fielding of candidates outside the Northern region, though the party members were dismayed such divisive attitude did not receive reciprocal treatment from the western and eastern Nigerian parties. Along with their motto, NPC also regarded other parties' campaigning in the Northern Region as assaults on its territorial sovereignty. This further fanned the embers of political instability on the fragmented polity.

Despite these unhealthy politicking, the region based parties paraded two assurances. First, that none of the parties will govern Nigeria on its own. Secondly that ethnic conflict was only a matter of time away[141]. Along with these assurances came the December 12, 1959 general election in which "no party was able to win a simple majority of the 312 seats in the Federal Legislature to enable it form a government"[142]. However, the two leading parties; Northern People's Congress (NPC) and National Congress of Nigeria and the Cameroons (NCNC) formed a coalition government, leaving Action Group (AG) in opposition. Alhaji Abubakar Tafawa Belewa became the Prime Minister, and Dr. Nnamdi Azikiwe became the President of the Senate, and later on November 10, 1960 became Governor General of Nigeria. When Nigeria became a Republic in 1963, Dr. Azikiwe became the first president of the Federal Republic of Nigeria. Since Nigeria was practicing a Federal Parliamentary system of government, all the executive powers reside, not with the President, but with the Prime Minister.

However, the first republic was bedeviled by several crises which the government could not manage. These crises among others include "the Western crises of 1962, the Nigerian census controversy of 1962 and 1963, the Federal election crises of 1964 and the Western Nigerian election crises of 1965."[143] At the root of these crises was ethnic politics deepened by erstwhile colonists' support of Northern region over other regions.

---

[141] Max Siollun, *Oil, Politics and Violence: Nigeria Military Coup Culture : 1966-1976* (New York: Algora Publishers, 2009), 12.

[142] Miriam Ikejiani-Clark, "Governor-Generalship/Presidency of Nigeria," in *Azikiwe and the African Revolution*, edited by M.S.O Olisa and Miriam Ikejiani- Clerk (Onitsha; Africana-Feb Publishers Ltd, 1989),245.

[143] J.O. Ojiako, *Nigeria: Yesterday, Today and ...?* (Onitsha: African Educational Publishers Ltd., 1981),3-4.

9.1.2 *The Military Juntas and Second Republic*

The political crises that erupted in Nigeria's first Republic was mainly ethnic based and was aggravated by the political elite's inability to see Nigeria from a patriotic point of view. Because of these raging crises and unpatriotic stance of the political elite, the military led by Majors Kaduna Nzeogwu, Ifeajuna and Ademoyega struck on January 15, 1966 through a *coup d'etat*. This coup later paved way for Major General Aguiyi Ironsi to become the Head of State. However, the coup fuelled more ethnic crises because the North thought it as an Igbo coup as they claimed they had more casualties than other regions. It could be recalled that the North had been wary of united Nigeria for it feels that the South will dominate it in a united Nigeria. This was why Nigerian independence was delayed till 1960 for Britain to convince the North to join the South as one Nigeria.

However, the unitary policy of the new Ironsi led military junta was resisted by the north. This unitary system came through Decree Nos. 33 and 34 of May 24, 1966. The promulgation of these decrees abolished political, ethnic and cultural associations that had once served as the platform for the aggregation of popular opinions. Although the enactments of these decrees were well intended, their timing was wrong.[144] More so, it fanned the embers of political instability on the already fragmented Nigerian polity. The resistance of these decrees by the north however became evident in the counter coup that toppled Ironsi administration and brought Lt. Col. Yakubu Gowon to power in July 1966. However, the military junta of Gowon stuck on to same one unitary policy that made him and his cohorts assassinate his predecessor. Thus, he completely abolished regional governments and put in place a unitary government.

With easterners being the victims of pogrom in the north, coupled with the apathy of Gowon led military junta towards the pogrom, a civil war that lasted from 1967 to 1970 broke out. Few years after the civil war, the government of Gowon was over thrown in a bloodless coup in July 29, 1975. The beneficiary of this coup was the 37 years old Brigadier General Murtala Muhammed who assumed the role of the Head of State. On Friday February 13, 1976, Lt. Colonel Burkar Suka Dimka led a mutiny that murdered Murtala Muhammed. General Olusegun Obasanjo became the Head of State and conducted a transition to democratic government.

The democratic government of Mallam Shehu Shagari that marked the second Nigerian republic was cut short in 1983 by a military coup that installed Major General Muhammed Buhari as the head of state. Buhari's government was toppled by another coup led by Major General Ibrahim Babangida who promised to inaugurate a democratic government. This was not to materialize as Babangida ruled with iron fist until 1993 when he gave room for a general election that was won by Moshood Abiola. Babangida cancelled the release of election results, constituted and handed over to an Interim National Government led by Ernest Shonekon. The interim government was brought to an end shortly by a silent coup led by General Sani Abacha who took over power and wanted to make himself a life President of Nigeria. After Abacha's

---

[144] Isaac Adegboyega, Ajayi. "Military Regimes and Nation Building in Nigeria, 1966-1999," in *African Journal of History and Culture*, vol. 5, no 7, (2013):138-142.

death in 1998, General Abdusalami Abubakar stepped in as the Head of State and within one year conducted a transition to the third Republican Government.

9.1.3 *Third Republic till Date*

After the general election of February 1999, Olusegun Obasanjo was elected the President of Nigeria. From May 29 when he was sworn in, the new republic was seen as a watershed in Nigerian history. This was because the administration moved to revive the economy and also began with new hope and expectation. Although progress was made and many democratic institutions were erected, the administration was marked and marred by corruption and misrule. After eight years of democratic rule, a general election brought in Mallam Shehu Musa Yar'dua as the President. The election was marked by massive rigging and irregularities. However, Yar'dua's regime was marred by his ill health which deprived him of concentration on state affairs. After his death midway into administration, his deputy Goodluck Jonathan was sworn in as a replacement.

A general election was then conducted in 2010 and Jonathan won overwhelmingly. The Goodluck Jonathan's administration under PDP was renowned for its massive corruption and administrative recklessness in all tiers of government. In 2014, a general election brought in General Muhammed Buhari as the president of Nigeria. Buhari came under the APC mantra of "change" and Nigerians expected much from his administration. The government of Muhammed Buhari dashed the expectations of Nigerians to the ground. This is as his government never brought any positive change. Rather, his cluelessness and incompetency in the management of the economy is daily taking Nigeria into economy depletion, recession and high inflation. This has resulted to job losses, government inability to pay workers, mass poverty, general hardship and low life expectancy. Worst, Buhari's government has brought more division and instability in the polity, rendered Nigeria a stateless state and aggravated the general call for restructuring of the country.

9.2 INHERITED COLONIAL STRUCTURE IN NIGERIAN POLITY

It is glaring that Nigerian present political systems did not stem from the indigenous peoples understanding and thoughts about politics. The systems were rather package and doled out to pristine Nigerian leaders at independence. In tracing the cradle of political instability in Nigeria, Ejiogu in his work, *The Root of Political Instability in Nigeria* alludes to some of the contents of this packaged colonial system. Hear him:

> My research indicates that political instability in Nigeria is not a post – colonial affair as orthodox studies claim. In fact, it shows that political instability in Nigeria entered another phase when colonial rule ended in 1960. British delivery of political power to the Hausa- Fulani through the rigged 1951-2 census and the 1959 elections did not help matters.[145]

---

[145] E.C Ejiogu,1 -21.

In congruence with this, Olusoji attests:

> there was no way in which the neo-colonial social formation inherited by Nigeria with its conditions of dislodgement, confusion, dependence, foreign domination, alienation of the people from the state, an unproductive and dependent dominant class and structural disabilities could have been stable or united following political independence on 1st October 1960.[146]

As such, the major change at independence was the replacement of colonisers with indigenous political stooges and collaborators. The sad story is that these replacements were manipulated and imposed on the people which sowed the seed of the culture of imposition of political candidates and policies on the masses. Based on these, post-independence Nigeria is characterized by colonial inherited structure seen in such systems as political manipulations, maneuverings, mediocrity (now embedded in Federal character), riggings, coercion, imposition of political candidates on the people, census manipulations, militarization politics, breach of human rights, divide and rule syndrome, indirect rule, and political instability.

Clearly, these inherited colonial systems are consciously packaged not to conform to the existent pattern of life among most indigenous Nigerian tribes and cultures. This is in order to retain the influence of the erstwhile colonists in Nigerian political space. Consequently, Akinola avers that post-independence Nigeria run "ready-made state disposing enormous power but with few virile institutions that could check the abuse of these powers."[147]

As such, there has been constant friction and conflict within the government circle in the verge to make this inherited political system functional among the indigenous Nigerian people. This has militarized Nigerian state and turned governance to coercive orders, combat rather than dialogue, disregard for rule of law, violation of human rights and political principles. Victims of this friction, on the other hand, do all it takes to redirect governance in accordance with their autochthonous pattern of life. And in expression of their grievances, there have been consistent upheavals visible in demonstrations, riots, violence, thwarting of political processes, etc. All these frictions and conflicts in all ramifications propel political instability in Nigeria.

9.3 ENDEMIC CORRUPTION IN NIGERIA

Corruption affects political stability and leadership in Nigeria. Indeed, a corrupt society is always that with political instability. This means that qualitative growth and development have always been an outcome in less corrupt society. The unchecked endemic corruption in Nigeria therefore largely contributes to incessant political instability in the country. This is as it destroys stable and conducive environment, image of the country, weakens trust and confidence,

---

[146] Olusoji, G. "Military Interventions in the Nigeria Politics: A 'time bomb' waiting to Explode? The Avowal of a New Management Elites," in *International Journal of Business, Humanities and Technology*, vol. 2, (2012): 195.
[147] Akinola, G. A. "Factors in the Development of a Democratic Ethics in Africa," in *Democracy, Democratization and Africa,* edited by Thomson, L.A. (Ibadan: Afrika Link, 1994),27.

compromises free, fair and efficient market, scares investors and tourists, reduces production, services and industry and robs government of national income that could have been channeled to meaningful development.[148] With these dire effects, Nigerian politics have been truncated and governance has remained a herculean task.

Thus, there is a strong link between corruption and the quality of leadership in Nigeria. Historically, the origin of corruption in Nigeria dates back to the colonial era. Before independence, there have been cases of official misuse of resources for personal enrichment. The colonial masters constructed the Nigeria state as a very powerful, absolute and arbitrary state. The violent character of colonial state placed it in a perpetual situation of war against the people.

Moreover, the colonial masters were more concerned with its exploitive mission than anything else. Thus, at the dawn of independence, the colonialists had to train and hand over power to agents who would continue to protect their colonial interests. These operators became profligate and went extra miles to enrich themselves. The realization that they needed economic power to retain political power made them even more profligate. So the people resent them, making their rule illegitimate. In order to legitimize their rule, besides the use of coercions, they had to use unethical means such as "settlements" among other unpopular measures.[149] The first Republic under the leadership of Sir Abubakar Tafawa Belewa, the Prime Minister, and Nnamdi Azikiwe, the President, was marked by widespread corruption. Government officials looted funds with impunity. Federal Representatives and Ministers flaunted their wealth with reckless abandon. In fact, it appeared there were no men of good character in the political leadership of the First Republic. Nigeria leadership class was based on politics for material gains, making money and living well. So the political leadership of Nigeria was founded on corruption and corruption has been the bane of political leadership till date.

Furthermore, a careful analysis of all the regimes of leadership in Nigeria from Independence till date reveals that leadership and corruption are positively correlated. This is based on the fact that almost all the leaders in Nigeria came to power with the sole purpose of enriching themselves and their cronies rather than offering selfless services to the country. The problem of Nigeria is bad leadership. Thus, Chinua Achebe argues:

> The trouble with Nigeria is simply and squarely a failure of leadership. There is nothing wrong with the Nigerian land or climate or water or air or anything else. The Nigerian problem is the unwillingness or inability of its leaders to rise to the responsibility, to the challenge of personal example which is the hall mark of true leadership.[150]

In continuation, Achebe insists that "Nigerians are corrupt because the system under which they live today makes corruption easy and profitable; they will cease to be corrupt when corruption

---

[148] Gregory Emeka, Chinweuba. "Low Level Corruption in Nigerian Society: A Critical Investigation," in *ORACLE OF WISDOM Journal of Philosophy and Public Affairs*, vol. 4, no. 1, (2020): 32-33.

[149] Micheal M. Ogbeidi, "Political Leadership and Corruption in Nigeria Since 1960: A Socio- Economic Analysis," in *Journal of Nigeria Studies*, vol. 1, no. 2, (2012):1-25.

[150] Chinua Achebe, *The Trouble with Nigeria* (England: Heinemann Educational Books, 1984), 1.

is made difficult and inconvenient."[151] Successive governments have put in place enabling anti-corruption laws. Obasanjo-led civilian government strengthened existing anti-corruption laws and established two important anti-corruption institutions. These are Independent Corrupt Practices Commission (ICPC) and Economic and Financial Crimes Commission (EFCC). These institutions hold the mandate to tackle the menace of corruption in public and private life squarely. But just as Achebe stated, neither exemplary leadership nor enabling environment is available for these institutions to function. They are rather used by politicians to fight their perceived political enemies or opponents.

Moreover, if we must have good leadership in the country then corruption has to be controlled. It is not that we cannot have bad leadership where there is no corruption. The argument is that bad leadership in Nigeria is positively correlated with corruption. And if corruption is controlled, there will be economic development of the country and of course political stability. So the leaders who are corrupt use ethnicity and religion as means of avoiding public scrutiny. Many of the ethnic and religious crises in Nigeria are indeed products of these maneuvers.

In congruence with the position of this discourse on corruption, Ene, et al, in their article "Corruption Control and Political Stability in Nigeria: Implication for Value Orientation in Politics", concur that political instability in Nigeria is as a result of the endemic corruption. According to them:

> Every informed person will agree that among many factors affecting political instability in Nigeria as well as most African countries, corruption has been the control factor. The crave by leaders and public servants in Nigeria to amass wealth while in public service, has not only affected national development but accentuated political instability.[152]

On the other hand, the issue of misplacement of values by Nigerians is greatly linked to the problems of bad leadership and corruption. Granted that our founding fathers have some failings, the present leaders cannot be compared to them. Hence, Ejiofor opines:

> In Nigeria, before the civil war, political parties and politicians were guided more or less by some unwritten code of conduct, which reflected the norms and values of Nigerian people.... Today the norms, values and ethos have changed. The sense of responsibility to the electorate has died down.[153]

The implication of this assertion is that our political system is getting worse every day because our leaders are not getting any better. Hence, Okolo did not agree with Achebe that

---

[151] Chinua Achebe,38.

[152] Ene I., et al., "Corruption Control and Political Stability in Nigeria: Implication for Value Orientation in Politics,"
in *Global Journal of Human Social Science,* vol. 13, (2013): 7- 12.

[153] Peter Ejiofor, "Dynamics of Party Politics in Democracy: The case of Nigeria," in *Church and Democracy in West Africa : Proceedings of the Conference of the Fourteenth CIWA Theology Week Held at the Catholic Institute of West Africa, 7 – 11 April, 2003,* edited by F. Nwigbo (Port Harcourt: CIWA Publications, 2003), 17 – 18.

the fundamental problem of democracy in Nigeria is bad leadership. The problem with Nigeria according to Okolo:

> Is the consumer or squandermania consciousness, essentially, the problem of value exhibited by both leaders and the led alike. This "consciousness" is easily defined as that disposition in a people by which conceive and judge things mostly in terms of their materialistic, at times, consumable values.[154]

This misplacement of values can be located in the people's excessive love for money, cheap popularity or fame, love for material labour and despotism.[155] Therefore, the whole political system of the country is sick because neither the leaders nor the led understand the true meaning of man's true self-worth and work. Hence both the issues of bad leadership and misplacement of values are to be tackled for there to be political stability in Nigeria.

9.4 UNHEALED WOUNDS OF THE CIVIL WAR

Because of the mutual suspicion between the North and the South, the first coup of 1966 was seen by the North as an Igbo ploy to dominate the Nigerian state. The counter-coup was therefore taken as a means of curtailing the excesses of the Igbo dominance in the Nigerian polity. If the Northern controlled Federal government had controlled the pogrom of the Southerners in the North, perhaps there would not have been a civil war.

According to Odumegwu Ojukwu:

> the people of Biafra feel very strongly that they were rejected from the erstwhile Federation of Nigeria. In that rejection they were brutalized. Those of us who were left in the area which is now Biafra only did what is natural in the circumstances - that was to create a home for our fleeing people to come back to."[156]

Truly, the Igbo have always been treated as a conquered tribe in post-civil war Nigeria. Although some people praised the effort of the Gowon led administration because of its policy of integration aimed at "binding up the nation's wound,"[157] many still see other polices such as the giving of 20 pounds to each Igbo who had money in the bank and claiming of Igbo properties in other parts of Nigeria as not actually binding the wound but as a message to the Igbo that they were conquered. Fifty years after the civil war, the Igbo have been on the receiving end of Nigeria's political instability: The Igbo have lesser states than other geographical zones in Nigeria, no Igbo has become the president of the country from the end of the war till date, the Igbo are

---

[154] Barnabas Okolo, *Education and Nigerian Values: A Companion for Students* (Enugu: Cecta(Nig) Ltd. 1993), 11-12.

[155] Okwudiba Nnoli, *Ethnic Politics in Nigeria* (Enugu: Fourth Dimension Publishing Co. Ltd. 1980), 79.

[156] Odumegwu Ojukwu, *Biafra: Random Thoughts (*New York: Harper& Row, Publishers, 1969), 25.

[157] Marthin Meredith, *The State of Africa* (UK: Simon and Schuster, 2011), 204.

shortchanged in recruitment exercises into the federal ministries and parastatals, civil, military and paramilitary services.

Thus, it is not a surprising that many youths in Igbo land are agitating for Biafra fifty years after the war. The Movement for the Actualization of the Sovereign State of Biafra (MASSOB), Indigenous People of Biafra (IPOB) and other such organizations are indeed fighting for the freedom of Biafra from Nigeria. Until the wounds of the civil war are healed through true reconciliation and restructuring, agitation for Biafra will continue to cause instability in the Nigerian polity.

9. 5 MILITARY INTERVENTIONS IN THE POLITY

The use of army personnel by the colonists to administer Nigeria remained a model for Nigerian politicians. Worst still, it presented a model of justification for some Nigerian military officers to intervene in Nigeria's politics. It is worthy of note that the first Governor General of Nigeria - Lord Lugard and some of his Governors were serving or retired British soldiers. Lugard studied at the Royal Military College, Sandhurst, United Kingdom. Most of the Nigerian senior military officers who participated in the various coups in Nigeria were trained at Sandhurst, and no doubt could have been interested in an old student like Lord Lugard"[158]. Also, despite the fact that Nigeria became a Republic in 1963, the Nigerian Armed Forces are still structured along the British Military system. And to implement British-oriented doctrines, most of the training of Nigerian soldiers was done in England and in British fashion. George Olusoji opines that:

the main reason why there was frequent military intervention in Nigeria is because there was no way in which the neo-colonial social formation inherited by Nigeria with its conditions of dislodgment, confusion, dependence, foreign domination, alienation of the people from the state, an unproductive and dependent dominant class and structural disabilities could have been stable or united following political independence on 1st October 1960.[159]

Moreover, many people believe that the military do not have what it takes to manage the affairs of the country. This is because most of the military personnel are not educated but were recruited in response to the defense urgencies that at intervals plague the country. Again, the military are always aware of their unpopularity hence each coup plotters was always quick in promising to hand-over to the civilian government as soon as practically possible. However, this is not to take away the contributions of the military towards the development of Nigerian polity.

The military have tried to bring stability to the polity through the creation of states, formulations and implementations of different economic policies and through the creation of such formulae like "Quota system" and "Federal character" in order to ensure some sort of balance in matters of admission or recruitment into public institutions and appointment in public offices.

---

[158] George Olusoji. "Military Interventions in the Nigeria Politics: A 'time bomb' waiting to Explode? The Avowal of a New Management Elites" In International *Journal of Business, Humanities and Technology*, vol. 2, no.5, (2012): 191-197.
[159] George Olusoji, 191- 197.

In theory, these policies appeared well intentioned and patriotically motivated but in practice, they are regularly manipulated to favour parochial interests.[160]

The greatest impact of frequent military role on the polity is seen in the militarized political culture, manifested in the political behavior of many Nigerian politicians. This erodes the civic culture and inculcates militarized culture in the public. As such, the rule of operation has become that of order and combat rather than dialogue, disregard of court orders, and the violation of human rights in the democratic dispensation. Worst still, there is dominance of ex-military men in Nigerian politics even as they are not yet civilized.[161] This and its resultant political instability are now at are peak in the present Buhari's APC led Federal Government.

9.6 ABSENCE OF POLITICAL AND ECONOMIC FREEDOM

There is a strong relationship between freedom and political stability. On the other hand, Malik Fahim Bashir and Changsheng Xu in their article, "Impact of Political Freedom, Economic Freedom and Political Stability on Economic Growth", add that "at present there is a near consensus in the literature that poor economic outcomes are often associated with lack of political stability and economic freedom."[162] In the same vein, Abdiweli Ali and Hodan Said Isse, in their article, "Political Freedom and Stability of Economic Policies", came in support of the argument that political freedom has strong effect on the political stability of any nation. They maintain that "the empirical results indicate that countries with high levels of political freedom tend to have more stable and durable economic policies."[163] These scholars indeed emphasize the importance of freedom to economic development.

9.7 THE NIGER DELTA QUESTION

Crude oil is the mainstay of Nigerian economy. This is as it accounts for over 90 percent of Nigerian revenue or national income. However, greater quantity of this crude oil is explored in the Niger Delta. Despite this, the inhabitants of the area wallow in poverty, isolation and infrastructural decadence. Therefore, the "paradoxical condition of the Niger Delta"[164] has to do with the fact that environmental degradation, poverty and unemployment have been on the increase in the Niger Delta region despite over fifty years of oil exploration. Today, the inhabitants

---

[160] Isaac Adegboyega Ajayi, 140.

[161] Frank O. Etim.and Wilfred Ukpere, "The Impart of Military Rule on Democracy in Nigeria," in *Journal of Social Sciences*, vol. 33, no. 3, (2012): 285-292.

[162] Malik Fahim Bashir and Changsheng Xu, "Impart of Political Freedom, Economic Freedom and Political Stability on Economic Growth," in *Journal of Economics and Sustainable Development*, vol.5, no.22, (2014): 59- 67.

[163] Ali Abdweli and Hodan Said Isse. "Political Freedom and Stability of Economic Policies," in *Cato Journal*, vol. 24, no.3, (2005): 251 – 260.

[164] Charles Nweke, "The Philosophy of Non-Violence and the Niger Delta Question," in *Journal of the Department of Philosophy*, Nnamdi Azikiwe University, Awka, Nigeria, vol..5, no.1, (2013): 50-64.

of Niger Delta have been reduced to a level below World Bank's benchmark as official figure places 72 percent of families in that area within poverty brackets.[165]

Consequently, the Niger Delta question has given rise to lots of issues such as agitation for resource control, youths restiveness as a result of unemployment and underdevelopment of their area, environmental degradation as a result of oil spillage and gas flaring, corruption among the Niger-Delta politicians, problem arising from the land use Act of Nigeria, militarization of the region and international interest in the area.[166] These issues have continued to bring instability into the Nigeria political and economic spaces. In this regard, Darlynton Okoye argues that:

> Since after the Kaiama declaration by over five thousand Ijaw youths representing over five hundred communities in Ijaw land and congregating in the birthplace of their national Hero, Isaac Adaka Boro, youth militancy in the Niger Delta region of Nigeria has spiraled almost beyond control even beyond the competent professionalism of the regular armed forces of Nigeria, who in turn appear to be handicapped by the circumstances that led other people to rebel against the federal might, in the fight in defense of the mutilation of their motherland.[167]

Thus, the glaring point is that with oil exploration in the Niger Delta, the area has been riddled with conflict of interests. This conflict is engineered by exploitation of the people by Nigerian government and oil companies who are driven by greed and selfish interest.

Apart from Nigerian government not rising up to its responsibility as regards the welfare of the Niger Delta people, the laxity and crookedness of the multinational oil companies in the region is also a serious matter of concern. These bodies instead of making effort to resolve crises in the region are interested in bribing leading figures to make decision that favour their business in the region.

The youth restiveness in the Niger Delta has metamorphosed into splinter militant groups such as the Niger Delta People Volunteer Force (NDPVF), Movement for the Emancipation of the Niger Delta (MEND), Niger Delta Avengers (NDA), etc. These militant groups are always involved in the kidnapping of foreign oil workers, fighting the Nigerian military, destroying oil installments, irregular refining/oil bunkering and all other activities meant to express their grievances. The activities of these militants are affecting the oil production of Nigeria. Since Nigeria's economy is oil based, the activities of these militants will continue to be a threat to the stability of Nigeria till their grievances are addressed.

---

[165] P. H Nmah, "Nigeria: Democracy, Human Rights and Niger Delta Issue," in *The Humanities and Nigeria's Democratic Experience*, edited by Chiegboka, A. B.C et al. (Nimo: Rex Charles & Patrick Ltd, 2009),171 - 174

[166] Dalynton Okoye, "Peace Support Organizations in Nigeria," in *Peace Studies and Conflict Resolution in Nigeria: A Reader*, edited by Miriam Ikejiani-Clark (Ibadan: Spectrum Book Ltd, 2009),250.

[167] Benson Igboin. "Boko Haram Fundamentalism: A Critical Metamorphosis," in *CJK*, vol. 3, no. 2, (2015): 72-96.

9.8 BOKO HARAM INSURGENCY

Boko Haram is an Islamic terrorist group that has expressed their desire for a strict conservative Islamic state and law in Nigeria. There are several theories that interpret the reason behind emergence of Boko Haram Insurgency in Northern Nigeria. According to Nkechi Anyadike:

> The theories are divided into two broad spectrums. One views the problem essentially as internal. The other blames external forces. The former looks at the socioeconomic factors, as well as deep-seated political, religious differences in the Nigerian society. It also includes vengeance over the death of the sect's leader, Ustaz Muhammed Yussuf. The external forces argument has two planks: One characterizes the problem as part of global Islamic Jihad and focuses on the sect's link with International terror groups such as al Qaeda or its affiliates as al Shahaab or the al Qaeda in the Islamic Maghreb (AQIM); the other views it as conspiratorial —a grand strategy to achieve the predicted disintegration of Nigeria in 2015.[168]

At the foundation of these theories is the grievance of the youths, who are isolated by the current system of government, and consequently look for any opportunity to escape from the harsh and hard condition of their environment. Moreover, Boko Haram is a combination of Hausa and Arabic words. "Boko" is an Hausa word which means "book" and "Haram" is an Arabic word which simply means "Forbidden".

Literally, Boko Haram means "Book is forbidden". It connotes "the rejection of Western education or civilization as forbidden, or as a normative evaluation, as bad, evil and sinful"[169]. This ideological basis though may not be justified within the context of the global contributions of Muslims to knowledge, it is in tandem with the argument that colonial construction of Nigeria is not favourable to the different components that make up the nation but only to the political elite who are satisfied with the *status quo*.

There are conflicting versions about the origin of Boko Haram. Many scholars traced this origin to sometime in 1995 and linked it with one Lawan Abubakar who later left for further studies at the University of Medina, Saudi Arabia. Under Abubakar, the sect was known as Sahaba. It was stated that Muhammed Yusuf to whom the formation is now generally ascribed to, only assumed leadership after Abubakar's departure.[170] The obscurity surrounding its origin perhaps informs why initially, the set had no specific name. This is as its members attracted several descriptions where they operated based on the local people's perception of them. The sect soon became formally identified as Ahulsunnawal'Jama'ah Hijra- "Congregation of Followers of the

---

[168] Benson Igboin. "Boko Haram Fundamentalism: A Critical Metamorphosis," in *CJK*, vol. 3, no. 2, (2015): 74-78.

[169] Nkechi Anyadike, "Boko Haram and National Security Challenges in Nigeria, Causes and Solutions," in *Journal of Economics and Sustainable Development*, vol. 4, no.5, (2013): 12-23.

[170] Ene, et al, "Corruption Control and Political Stability in Nigeria: Implication for Value Re-Orientation in Politics,"
in *Global Journal of Human Social Science*, vol. 13,(2013):7-12.

Prophet Involved in the Call to Islam and Religious Struggle". The name Boko Haram to which it is now commonly referred to derives from the sect's anti-Western posturing.

Although, Yussuf allegedly drew inspiration from a radical Islamist Ibn Taymiyya, he reportedly resisted the move by followers to resort to violence as a means of achieving their ideal Islamic state. He was said to be against any form of violence, saying it was against the teaching of Islam. But it is still unclear whether the sect's current level of radicalization is a function of the deaths of its initial leadership and subsequent clampdown by the state or the accession to its leadership of Abubakar Shekau, a taciturn psychopath. Indeed, the organization is trying to create a "state" within the Nigerian State.

They have attacked government facilities, churches, and market places and kidnapped many people. They use sophisticated weapons and suicide bombers during the attack. Indeed, the attack of Boko Haram in the North East has reduced that zone to a shadow of itself and is affecting the political stability of Nigeria. Consequently, Nigerian security has been stretched beyond its bounds, the economy is also affected and the security of life and property not only in North East but in the entire Nigeria is being jeopardized.

As earlier stated, at the foundation of the group's agitation is their belief that the state of hopelessness in their region was caused by government, which imposed western education on them and failed to manage the resources of the country to their benefits. At this initial stage, the government of the day failed to curtail the group but politicized it for political gains. And when the government of Goodluck Jonathan wanted to handle the situation, he was sabotaged by some northern elements in his government. Of course, the problem of Boko Haram insurgency in Nigeria cannot be treated or solved in isolation to the myriad of problems beseeching the nation as a result of defaulted political structure of Nigeria.

CHAPTER TEN

TOWARDS POLITICAL STABILITY OF NIGERIA

10.1 JUSTIFICATION OF FANON'S DIALECTICS OF FREEDOM IN NIGERIA'S SITUATION

In the light of increasing crises and quagmire in which Nigeria has found herself, it becomes pertinent to explore how Frantz Fanon's theory of freedom – dialectics of freedom, can be adapted as a paradigm for political stability in Nigeria. This is more so because there are similarities between Fanon's colonial world and Nigeria's political situation. Both are characterized by violence as a result of the exploitation of the colonized by colonizers in Fanon's world, and the masses by the political elite in Nigerian situation. Also both situations consist of a binary world of the colonizers and the colonized and political elite and the masses. And more so, the Nigerian political elite are more of replacements of the colonial masters. In Frantz Fanon's dialectics of freedom however, the synthesis of freedom would always be anticipated in the dialectical relations between the thesis of colonialism and the antithesis of anti-colonial struggles.

10.2 DIALECTICS OF FREEDOM AS A PARADIGM FOR POLITICAL STABILITY IN NIGERIA

This research tries to demonstrate that the main reason why there is political instability in Nigeria is the inherited colonial structure in the Nigerian's political system. The argument has been that it is only through a change of paradigm from colonial to anti-colonial, that political stability will be achieved in Nigeria. The anti-colonial paradigm is best represented by Fanon in his dialectics of freedom. In this section, effort will be made to apply the adaptable principles of Fanon's dialectics of freedom into Nigerian's political situation. The general approach will be to examine the present political situation in Nigeria in the light of the features of dialectics of freedom in Frantz Fanon, with a view to finding out how the features of dialectics of freedom can proffer solutions to political instability in Nigeria.

10.2.1 *Colonisation and Decolonisation*

At the heart of Frantz Fanon's dialectics of freedom is the movement of the colonised from colonisation to decolonisation. Fanon has warned that unless real decolonisation is achieved the flag independence got by the African States will usher in another form of colonisation-neo-colonization. This eventually happened in Nigeria as the colonial structure, exemplified by the colonial constitution and the unpreparedness of the political and intellectual elites who should have played an important role as agents of decolonisation has continued to exist in Nigeria six decades after independence. It is only when the elite play an active role in the anti-colonial struggle that there will be real decolonization. Fanon was quick to note that the political elite that took over power at the end of colonial regime is an undeveloped political elite because it has practically no economic power and in any case, it is in no way commensurate with the bourgeoisie of the mother country which it hopes to replace.[171] Thus, the political elite are contented with replacing the colonial masters than in changing the colonial structure, which it neither had the will nor the wherewithal to effect.

In continuation, the colonial structure of Manichaean division of society into two continues to exist in Nigeria. The division has been between the political elite, who have benefitted inordinately from the structure and the masses who have been the victims of maladministration. Because the political elite are not ready to change the *status quo*, Nigeria has careered from British colonisation to internal colonisation. The politicians have become the masters and the masses have been turned into slaves. Just as Fanon predicted, the elite have continued to serve the interest of the colonial masters even after independence. Nigeria like other independent African countries is therefore battling with two enemies of decolonisation since independence: the colonial masters, who are indirectly controlling the economy of the country to their advantage and the elite who have made themselves worthy instruments to further impoverish their fellow country men and women for their own advantage and those of the colonial masters.

Furthermore, the Nigeria's political situation illustrates the dual economy and divided worlds theory as Fanon posited regarding uneven and unequal development conditions that exist simultaneously with issues such as poverty and malnutrition. According to Njideka Odera Nnamdi, Nigeria's huge wealth gap depicts the continuation of the colonial legacy of preferential treatment to certain geographical regions. There is a clear socio-economic disparity between the poorer Muslim North and wealthier Christian South. These inequalities lead to the incitement of old pre-colonial rivalries and tribal hatred. The recent insecurity in Northern Nigeria and Islamic insurgency of Boko Haram are simply manifestations of the socio-economic disparity and regional favoritism in the Nigeria's polity.

The issue is that the political elite cash into these problems as opportunities to confuse, manipulate and further impoverish the masses. It is because the political elite are not prepared to play active role in the decolonization process that Fanon has given the major role of bringing about real decolonization to the masses. According to Fanon:

It is clear that in the colonial countries the peasant alone are revolutionary, for they have

---

[171] Fanon Frantz, *The Wretched of the Earth* trans. Constance Farrington (London: Penguin Books, 2001),120.

nothing to lose and everything to gain. The starving peasant, outside the class system, is the first among the exploited to discover that only violence pays. For him, there is no compromise, no possible coming to terms. Colonization and decolonization are simply a question of relative struggle."[172]

Fanon had earlier described decolonization as "always a violent phenomenon". The role Fanon attributes to violence in decolonization process is a slippery and delicate one and some people have misunderstood him. At the centre of his argument for the use of violence in decolonization is that colonization is always a violent situation and it is only a violent action that can destroy it, and that the violence of decolonization should always be equal to that of colonization. He is also insistent on the fact that violence is only a means and not an end to decolonization. Thus, although violence may not be the solution to colonization but an element of violence, even if it is resistance or civil disobedience, is always needed in decolonization.

The Nigerian masses have been exploited to the extent that it could be said that the masses have become passive to the political situation in Nigeria. The politicians are manipulating the masses for their own selfish interest. How can the masses be mobilized as effective agents of decolonization in Nigeria? Fanon provides the answer. According to him, "to educate the masses politically is to make the totality of the nation a reality to each citizen. It is to make the history of the nation part of the personal experience of each of its citizens."[173] The first task before any serious government is the education of its citizens. The kind of education that Fanon advocated is more of education in civic responsibility. This is carried out not only through dissemination of ideas but also through creating of enabling environment for the masses to participate in political activities.

But it is difficult for the same politicians that know that empowering the masses will bring their privileged positions to a halt to engage in the education of the masses.

On this, Fanon acknowledges that there is a sincere section of the intellectual elite who can create this awareness for the masses. In Nigeria many political activists, intellectuals, religious leaders and others who are not comfortable with the situation are already educating the masses politically. We see the role some intellectuals played to stop the government of Goodluck Jonathan from removing oil subsidy by mobilizing the masses against the government. Also, a mass movement, "Our Mumu Don Do", was able to force President Buhari to return home after he was away for more than hundred days on sick vacation in London. And the "#End SARS, End SWAT, End Corruption and Poor Governance Campaign#" against the clueless and despotic administration of President Muhammadu Buhari, which has spread through Nigerian cities and championed by the ordinary masses is another viable instance in this context.

The point is that it is only the masses that can free the country from neo-colonisation through active participation in political activities of the country. It is not enough that the masses be educated but they "must get angry" with the internal colonization in Nigeria and fight for their freedom. To say that the masses must get angry with the political situation in Nigeria is not to advocate the type of violence described by Fanon, although violence can only be a means not an

---

[172] Fanon Frantz, *The Wretched of the Earth*, 47.
[173] Fanon Frantz, *The Wretched of the Earth*, 161.

end to freedom, but to mean that the masses must have the political will to pursue the change of the situation. This is where Fanon's call for education of the masses can serve as an inspiration and solution.

10.2.2 *Ethnic Nationalism and National Consciousness*

The dialectics of race and negritude in Fanon leads either to ethnic nationalism or national consciousness. Unfortunately for Nigeria, the independence leads more to ethnic nationalism rather than national consciousness. Nationalism within the African context simply refers to patriotic feeling or effort or the act of political awareness or consciousness of the colonized people towards freedom from imperial rule. According to Osimen Goddy Uwa, et al:

> Nigeria nationalism by the 1940s was already facing regional and ethnic problems to its goal of promoting a united, Pan-Nigerian nationalism. Nigeria nationalism was geographically significant and important in Southern Nigeria while a comparable Nigerian nationalist organization did not arrive in Northern Nigeria until late 1940s.[174]

Hence, because of the divide-and-rule policy of the colonial government, ethnic politics played out in Nigeria during the colonial era. Even when the nationalists organized themselves to fight for independence, they did so more as ethnic nationalists rather than national nationalists.

Thus, there is no foundation for national consciousness at independence and ethnic politics became the bane of Nigerian politics till the present time. Both the political parties and the politicians have continued to advance regional and ethnic interests at the expense of the overall interest of Nigeria. Fanon traced the origin of ethnic nationalism to the laziness of the political elite. According to him:

> National consciousness, instead of the long all-embracing crystallization of the innermost hopes of the whole people, instead of being the immediate and the more obvious result of the mobilization of the people, will be in any case only an empty shell, a crude and fragile travesty of what it might have been. The faults that we find in it are quite sufficient explanation of the fault with which, when dealing with young and independent nations, the nation is passed over for the race and the tribe is preferred to the state.[175]

In continuation, Fanon was clear that the cause of ethnic politics in Africa can be traced both to the colonial masters and African political elite. According to Fanon, "colonialism, which has been shaken to its foundations by the birth of African unity, recovers its balance and tries now to break that will to unity by using all the movement's weaknesses. Colonialism will set the African

---

[174] Osimen, Goddy Uwa, et al, "Ethnicity and Identity Crisis: Challenge to National Integration in Nigeria, in *Journal of Humanities and Social Science*, vol. 16, Issue 4, (2013): 79-83.
[175] Fanon Frantz, *The Wretched of the Earth*, 119.

peoples moving by revealing to them the experience of spiritual rivalries.[176] The colonial masters' work with the political elite to bring disunity among the Nigerian people as instability will favour the colonial interest more than stability. The recent political happenings in the country where the West and America favoured President Buhari to the candidature of Goodluck Jonathan to become the President of Nigeria speak more about colonial interest and the use of ethnicity to destabilize Nigeria.

Both Britain and America, with collaborations from some Nigeria's politicians were more interested in returning power to the North than on the competencies of the candidates who were contesting for the 2015 presidential election. Also three years into President Buhari's regime, the government has nothing to offer Nigeria but the same western neo-colonial influence, ethnic sentiment and politics played out and brought him back to power in 2019.

Inculcating of national consciousness in the masses particularly as advocated by Fanon can enhance a rebirth of patriotism amongst Nigerians and liberate the country from her political instability. The issue is that a nation can be said to be stable when there is a program which has being worked out by revolutionary leaders and intellectuals and taken up with full understanding and enthusiasm by the masses. Apart from proposing political education for the masses, Fanon also sees the solution to ethnic nationalism on the participation of the masses in political activities and creating strong ideologies by the political elite and the intellectuals. Indeed, Fanon argues that the dialectics of race and negritude should move African countries to national consciousness. But national consciousness is a step to decolonisation. So, if one really wishes his or her country to avoid regression or to stand still, then a rapid step must be taken to move the country from national consciousness to political and social consciousness.[177]

10.2.3 *Identity Crisis and National Identity*

The dialectics of language and desire, and of self and other, are about the relationship between the individual and the society in a colonial world. The colonial world tries to turn the black into white. This is why Fanon proclaims that to be white is the desire of the black. The desire to be white brings about an identity crisis into the consciousness of the black. Identity crisis is when one either loses track of who he or she is or does not feel happy with who he or she is and wants to change one's life or restructure it.[178] The colonial world has made the black to desire to be white. But has the drive towards decolonisation healed the identity crisis in the consciousness of the African? Fanon has proposed the solution to identity crisis by maintaining that the African should go back to himself or herself in order to experience a mutation of the consciousness, which will set him free from the acquired inferiority complex.

In fact, coming back to oneself is the only option for the African as he or she realizes that he or she cannot be white. Also Fanon argues that Africa has to go back to her roots, past and cultural values. This going back will not be to admire the past but see how these cultural values are relevant to Africa's quest for freedom and her desire for a new humanity. But after independence,

---

[176] Fanon Frantz, *The Wretched of the Earth*, 128.
[177] Fanon Frantz, *The Wretched of the Earth*, 163.
[178] Osimen Goddy Uwa et al, 79-86.

many African countries are yet to come to terms with the fact that they are free. Many African states still want to be white. This is why President Trump had on few occasions maintained that Africa needed to be re-colonized.

In Nigeria, this crisis of identity is evident in different aspects of the people's life. The Nigerian elite are so desirous to be like the white man that they daily sacrifice the welfare of their fellow countrymen in order to achieve this dream. The Nigerian leaders are embezzling public funds in order to stash them in foreign banks or use them to acquire properties in foreign lands. The amount of money stashed in foreign banks by Nigerian politicians is more than enough to rebuild the economy of Nigeria. Nigeria youths are daily surging out of Nigeria to foreign lands believing that life is better lived in those countries. Many Nigerian youths are languishing in foreign prisons and many have been sold to different companies and agents in their quest to find greener pastures in those countries. Many of our intellectuals have refused to come back to Nigeria after their studies and training in foreign lands because they are afraid they cannot survive the hard and rough conditions of Nigeria. Some intellectuals, who eventually came back are so overwhelmed by the political situation that they enter into their cocoon and decide to be observers rather than contributors to national issues.

Equally, it has been noted that as colonial languages are still standing as the lingua franca in many African states, especially in Nigeria, coupled with western styled education curriculum, the psyche and destiny of the Africans are still controlled by the West.[179] Thus, the present educational system and curriculum are still tailored towards the colonial ideal of making Africans to be civilized instead of solving their immediate and pressing problems. And of course our hospitals are so bad that many of our elites travel outside the country for Medicare instead of investing to revive our health sector. The Covid – 19 pandemic demonstrated to a great extent the deplorable condition of health facilities and system in Africa. Can African leaders learn from the pandemic? I doubt they can. Also, many companies in Nigeria are still managed by expatriates and our engineers are there wasting and rusting away. At the root of the crisis of identity in Nigeria is the general belief that we cannot do it on our own or that ours is not good enough. The general notion is that we require the assistance of the white people to help in solving our problems. Unfortunately, the reality of international politics is that the big countries are only interested in countries they can benefit from.

The crises of identity can be overcome when there is a serious drive towards national integration. When the nationalists were fighting for independence, they had a dream of a united and prosperous nation where they would all live as brothers and sisters. Unfortunately, ethnic nationalism was able to suffocate the initial national consciousness that drove these men and women to fight the colonial masters to a standstill. Today more than ever, national integration is needed to bring about the desired unity and stability needed for the country to be prosperous and independent. Fanon has always insisted that the success of decolonization lies in a whole social structure being changed from the bottom to up. Today, this change of the social and political structure of Nigeria is the same as the general call for restructuring. It is the restructuring of the

---

[179] Evaristus Emeka Isife, "Dialectics of Freedom in Frantz Fanon and its Relevance in Contemporary Africa," in *IGWEBUIKE: An African Journal of Arts and Humanities*, vol. 6, no. 9,(2020): 118 - 131.

structure that will create the environment for national integration and national identity. Although the clamor for restructuring in Nigeria has been loud of recent, the most important thing about it which Fanon stressed is for it to be people oriented. The more people participate in it the more it will be successful. The restructuring should focus on the constitution of the country, cultural and human values and the aspirations of different nationalities in Nigeria. Restructuring of Nigeria will bring about national integration and national integration will bring about national identity. It is when Nigeria's identity crisis is overcome using Fanon's prescriptions as proffered above that political stability and economic prosperity can be attained.

10.2.4 *Invisibility and Active Participation*

The main point in the dialectics of visibility and invisibility in a colonial setting is that as the colonizer tries to make the colonized to be visible in order to dominate him or her, the colonized fights back by trying to be invisible. And also, as the colonizer attempts to make the colonized to be invisible by limiting his space, then the colonized tries to be visible by fighting for an increased political space, and eventually trying to take the place of the colonizer. This dialectics still plays out in the present Nigeria's political system where the political elite try to limit the masses from participating in political activities. But there cannot be political stability in Nigeria unless there is active participation of the masses in political activities. The intellectuals have a great role to play in this regard. Fanon, like Karl Marx before him, understands the relation between intellectuals and the masses as dialectical. The intellectuals should mobilize the masses for political actions, and the masses through their struggles and experiences should always provide the intellectuals with materials for better ideologies. The future remains a closed book so long as the masses are not conscious of what is happening around them. According to Fanon:

> The duty of those at the head of the movement is to have the masses behind them. Allegiance presupposes awareness and understanding of the mission which has to be fulfilled; in short, an intellectual position, however embryonic. We must not voodoo the people, nor dissolve them in emotion and confusion. Only those under-developed countries led by revolutionary elites who have come up from the people can today allow the entry of the masses upon the scene of history.[180]

It is the argument of Fanon that an individual's political experience gathered from participation in political activities, because it is natural and has a link in the chain of national existence, ceases to be individual, limited and shrunken and is enabled to open out into the truth of the nation and of the world.[181] But in Nigeria, the masses do not largely participate in politics. The root of non-participation of the masses in politics can be traced to the nationalists who contrary to Fanon's ideology did not allow the masses to participate in the struggle to decolonize and democratize

---

180 Fanon Frantz. *The Wretched of the Earth*, 161.
181 Fanon Frantz. *The Wretched of the Earth*, 161

the country[182]. Also, a factor that has hindered the masses from active participation in Nigerian politics is that of cultural systems denoting group boundaries in class and ethnicity. Nigerians usually base their participation on class and ethnicity. This problem is preventing people from involving themselves in honest and objective participation and has led to many people becoming uninterested in politics. In this vein, participation is based on class and ethnic considerations and not on the Nigerian nation building project.[183]

Moreover, there are other factors that militate against active participation of the masses in politics or rather to become visible as Fanon posits. These include: high rate of poverty in the country, a situation where people are battling for their daily bread and can easily be manipulated by greedy politicians, high rate of corruption among the politicians which makes the masses believe that their participation will not change anything in the political system, carpet crossing from one party to another by politicians, male domination and elite driven politics, militarization of the psyche of the people and the system which discourage dialogue and compromise, and of course political violence. In the last presidential election in Nigeria, less than 20% of registered voters participated in the election. The percentage is less in other elections. Of course, a greater percentage of those who are qualified to vote have not registered and do not have voter's cards.

The issue is that it is only when a greater number of people participates in political activities that there will be political stability in the country.

Furthermore, it is generally agreed that public participation in political activities helps to empower the masses. When ordinary citizens are involved in the process of decision making, it helps to generate superior solutions as a result of wider deliberation and the existence of multiple strategies to solving problems. Public participation removes bureaucracy and provides an opportunity for the ordinary citizens to have firsthand knowledge of government and citizenship education.

One of the foremost means of fostering national integration in Nigeria, a country that is battered by ethnicity and cries of marginalization from all sectors is to have mass participation of the populace in governance. Also, respect and sanctity of the ballot boxes, presence of transparent and responsible administration, robust civil societies, media and increased participation of women will encourage public participation of Nigerians in the political activities of the country. Public participation is an integral part of political education that is advocated by Fanon as a means of bringing about true decolonization of any country. Just as invisibility of the colonized perpetuated the colonial regime, the invisibility or apathy of the Nigerian populace will perpetuate elite dominance and corruption. To stop elite political process, Fanon therefore calls to the oppressed, and by extension the Nigerian masses, to be visible, to participate actively in politics, becomes a desideratum and solution.

---

[182] E. O. Adeoti and S. B. Olaniyan. "Democratization and Electoral Process in Nigeria: A Historical Analysis," in *International Journal of Multidisciplinary Approach*, vol. 1, no. 1, (2014): 1-13.

[183] Sulaimon Adigun Muse and Sagie Narsiah. "Challenges to Public Participation in Political Processes in Nigeria," in *Journal of Social Science*, vol. 44, no. 2,3, (2015): 181-187.

10.2.5 *Violence and Freedom*

Fanon proposes dialectics of violence within the context of anti-colonial struggle. According to him, violence is a necessary ingredient of liberation without which there is no genuine freedom. Fanon shares the same view with Sartre that dialectics is the practical consciousness of an oppressed class struggling against its oppression. According to Fanon, "the violence of the colonial regime and the counter-violence of the native balance each other and respond to each other in an extraordinary reciprocal homogeneity."[184] Many have criticized the role that Fanon assigned to violence in decolonization but some of them missed the point Fanon was trying to prove that "the development of violence among the colonized people will be proportionate to the violence exercised by the threatened violence of the colonial regime.[185]

If the colonial world is not violent, then there would be no need for violence on the part of the colonized. Thus, the two arguments that will always support the necessity of violence in the colonial world are the argument of "self-defense"[186] and that of "violence as a means to an end, not as an end to itself."[187] So, the concept of violence has to be expanded or stressed further for Fanon's dialectics of violence to be appreciated all the more. It is not just political violence but revolutionary violence geared towards the freedom of man.

Although the era of colonialism has elapsed, Africans, especially Nigerians, are being re-colonized through productive activities of external imperialists and African elites. It is a fact which is noted by Fidelis Chuka Aghamelu and Emeka Cyril Ejike who argue that:

The free penetration of imperialists' oligopolies into African nations and their alliance with African governments in this age of mercantilism are responsible for political, social and economic woes of Africans. The phenomena associated with imperialism which include, inter alia, economic and political hegemony, oppressive state machinery, militarism, enslavement and exploitation of indigenous population and racism are intrinsic features of colonialism which Fanon frowned upon and fought against."[188]

In Nigeria, the inherited colonial structures are evident in widespread violence in Nigeria as seen in violence in Niger-Delta area, the Boko Haram violence in Northern Nigeria, the herdsmen violence and other violent incidences in the country. At the foundation of this violence is the violence created by the political structure that favours the elite and pushes the masses to the fringe of existence. But the issue is that although the dialectics of violence is still relevant to Nigerian political situation, it cannot be applied as it is but should be adapted to the Nigerian political situation.

---

[184] Fanon Frantz, *The Wretched of the Earth*, 69.

[185] Fanon Frantz, *The Wretched of the Earth*, 69

[186] Richard Onwuanib,. *A Critique of Revolutionary Humanism: Frantz Fanon* (U.S.A: Warren H. Green, Inc., 1983),
60.

[187] Hussein Abdulahi Bulham, *Frantz Fanon and the Psychology of Oppression* (London: Plenum Press, 1985), 146.

[188] Fidelis Chuka Aghamelu and Emeka Cyril Ejike, "Understanding Fanon's Theory of Violence and its Relevance to Contemporary Violence in Africa," in *IGWEBUIKE: An African Journal of Arts and Humanities*, vol. 3, no.4,(2017): 22-44.

The aspect of violence that is important to Nigeria is positive violence or non-violent resistance, which has to do with aggressive participation of the masses in the political activities of the country. The masses should be angry with their condition in order to work towards changing it. The masses should develop the political will to change the situation.

The present situation in the country is such that the masses are suffering and smiling. But the masses should be sober and concerned about their welfare.

The non-violent resistance as advocated by Mahatma Gandhi and Martin Luther King Jnr. involves some positive aspects of violence. So, the masses should be aware of their power to change their condition and use it adequately. In this way, the deep lessons of Fanon's dialectics of violence and freedom will be deployed towards Nigeria's political development.

CHAPTER ELEVEN

EVALUATION AND CONCLUSION

11. 1 EVALUATION

It is because Fanon believes that colonialism has a strong philosophical foundation that he goes on to construct the dialectics of freedom as an anti-colonial philosophy that can lead to the freedom of the African and ultimately to a new humanity. According to Fanon, the colonial situation is already a term in the dialectical process (thesis), the reaction of the African to colonialism after an unsuccessful assimilation is another term (antithesis), and the destruction and transcending of the colonial situation leads to the final term of the dialectics – the synthesis. Colonialism brings a dividing line between the colonizers and the colonized but freedom is about transcending this dividing line.[189] Freedom comes when the colonized fights against his domination and subjugation in the colonial situation. The task before the colonized is to fight for the destruction of the colonial situation and liberate both himself or herself and the colonizer. When freedom is achieved, then a new humanity is created; one free from racism.

Freedom for Fanon has two dimensions; personal freedom and national freedom. Since colonial situation is built on violence, it can only be destroyed through violence. But Fanon believes there are two kinds of violence: the criminal violence being perpetuated by the colonizer against the colonized and the revolutionary violence against the colonizer. According to Fanon, the violence directed against the oppressor or the colonizer loses its criminal character because it is meant to liberate both the colonizer and the colonized. This is why it is called revolutionary violence. The personal freedom involves doing violence to self. Hence, according to Fanon, it is assured through the application of the psyche of assent suggested by Cesaire. This is what Fanon described as a "descent into a real hell" or a "leap into the black hole" of consciousness.[190] But national freedom is realized through an organized violence against the colonial situation. This organized violence is what Fanon calls violence in action or praxis.

The two dimensions of freedom are related and cannot be accomplished without each other. According to Fanon, "an authentic national liberation exists only to the precise degree to which

---

[189] Fanon Frantz, *A Dying Colonialism,* trans. Haakon Chevalier (New York: Grove Press, 1965), 32.
[190] Fanon Frantz, *Black Skin, White Masks,* trans. Charles Lan Markmann (London: Plato Press, 2008), 2 & 154.

the individual has irreversibly begun his own liberation."[191] The role of violence in Fanon's dialectics of freedom is very contentious. Fanon has tried to prove the necessity of violence in the colonial situation. But he was not able to prove how far violence can go in achieving the freedom of the colonized. Nor was he able to prove that violence which was started against colonialism would not continue when colonialism has been destroyed.

Although Fanon did not live to see the end of the Algerian Revolution or to revise his theory on violence, experience has always shown that violent actions are not always as positive as Fanon painted them to be. Thus, revolutionary activities are always unpredictable; they are like a leap in the dark which can be successful or unsuccessful depending on the circumstances.

Furthermore, an important task Fanon set before himself was to prove to the Africans that Algeria's revolution should serve as a paradigm to other African states. According to Fanon, the process of liberation of colonial peoples is indeed inevitable. But the form given to the struggle of the Algerian people is such that in its violence and in its total character, it will have a decisive influence on the future struggle of other colonies.[192] Of course, Algeria is paradigmatic because the struggle for freedom in Algeria has shown that freedom from colonial control is not free but has to be fought for. Nigeria is a country where people find it difficult to sacrifice for their country. It is a lesson that there will not be freedom in Nigeria till the people are educated or enlightened enough to know the importance of freedom and begin to fight for it. Although Nigeria got her independence more than five decades ago, the colonial structure is still imbedded in the political system. So, the Algerian experience is relevant to Nigeria as long as there is no political stability in the country.

Therefore, the main argument of this book is that the primary cause of Nigerian instability is the inherited colonial political structure. Before now, Fanon has already in *Black Skin, White Masks*, advocated that freedom can only come through the elimination of the "poison" of the inferiority complex inherited from colonialism and the restructuring of the colonial structure. This book contends that for Nigeria to be free and stable, there must be a change of political paradigm from the colonial to anti-colonial paradigm. This can be done primarily through restructuring of the mentality of Nigerians and the political system of Nigeria. Freedom begins from self-awareness and restructuring should begin with individuals. If individuals realize the need for them to be free, then restructuring the system will be easy.

And restructuring the system will destroy the unitary system inherited from the colonial masters and bring in a true federalism that will devolve powers among the components units of Nigeria and allow each unit to grow at its pace. Restructuring will also destroy the divide and rule principle introduced by the colonial masters and institutionalized by the military juntas which has become the bane of Nigerian democracy. When Nigeria is restructured, then other causes of instability will be taken care of since they are part of the problems of the inherited colonial structure. The reaction from some favoured elite against the move towards restructuring has shown that the struggle for restructuring will be like fighting for second independence of Nigeria. It is not going to be easy but it will take the enlightening of the masses for it to succeed.

---

[191] Fanon Frantz, *Towards the African Revolution*, trans. Haakon Chevalier (New York: Grove Press, 1967), 103.
[192] Fanon Frantz, *Towards the African Revolution*, 104.

Of course, the political elite are always afraid of the masses and take every measure to isolate the masses from political participation. Fanon reminds us of the importance of enlightened masses towards freedom.

Indeed, there has to be true freedom before we can talk about political stability. Hence, political stability would be realizable in Nigeria when the people decide to fight for their freedom. Political freedom when attained will bring about economic advancement which will eventually lead to political stability. Thus, political freedom is not got on a platter of gold; it has to be fought for. It is also a process and, as dialectics of freedom shows, political freedom involves some contradictions which will change both the system and the people and bring about a new Nigeria.

11. 2 CONCLUSION

There are two important ways in which Fanon's dialectics of freedom can become a paradigm for Nigerian political stability. These are: the need for a strong ideology for Nigerians and the orientation and education of the masses. In the first case, Fanon insists that "the nation does not exist except in a programme, which has been worked out by revolutionary leaders and taken with full undertaking and enthusiasm."[193] The revolutionary leaders can only come about through the restructuring of the country. When Nigeria is restructured, then the people will decide on how many political parties will be needed. And each political party will have a strong ideology which will eventually bring about good leaders and strong institutions. It means that before a person gets the ticket to contest any post under any political party, the aspirant or candidate should have been one who is trusted to make a good leader. So the value of leadership should be a serious concern for Nigeria if the country is to achieve the desired political stability.

On the other hand, Fanon argues that the revolutionary power resides with the masses. It is the masses that will fight for freedom. The problem of Nigerian democracy has been that the Nigerian masses are not always informed or educated properly on the real issues in Nigeria politics. Thus, Fanon argues that "to educate the masses politically is to make the totality of the nation a reality to each citizen."[194] The government should create opportunities for the masses to be educated. The National Orientation Agency should be empowered more to educate the people on what are their duties in the democratic settings and the need for active participation in democracy. The general apathy of the masses towards participation during elections and other political activities shows that greater percentage of the masses are ignorant or uninformed about the political happenings in the country. Greater effort should therefore be devoted by the government and other agencies in teaching of civic education to the students and the youths.

Finally, the change of paradigm spoken about also involves a change of attitude or the restructuring of the self. We can have the best system but if we do not change our attitude, it will not work. Re- orientation should involve the teaching of values that will bring positive attitudinal changes to Nigerians. The government should always celebrate role models, and not rogues, to

---

[193] Fanon Frantz, *The Wretched of the Earth*, trans. Constance Farrington (London: Penguin Books, 2001), 164.
[194] Fanon Frantz, *The Wretched of the Earth*, 61.

encourage the youths to aspire high. Our educational system should emphasize high values of honesty, sincerity, sacrifice and patriotism. Education should be given a pride of place in Nigeria. And Nigerian education system should focus more on technology and skill acquisition so that the country can achieve technological breakthrough, which is the bulwark of modern states.

BIBLIOGRAPHY

Achebe, Chinua. *The Trouble with Nigeria*. England: Heinemann Educational Books, 1984.

Adele, Jinadu. *Fanon: In Search of the African Revolution*. Enugu: Fourth Dimension Publishers, 1980.

——————————, "Review of Frantz Fanon: A Critical Study by Irene Gendzier." In *The Journal of Developing Areas*, vol. 8, no. 2,(1974): 300 -303.

——————————,"Some Aspects of the Political Philosophy of Frantz Fanon." In *African Studies Review*, vol. 16, no.2, (1973):255 – 289.

Adeoti, E. O. and Olaniyan, S. B. "Democratization and Electoral Process in Nigeria: A Historical Analysis." *In International Journal of Multidisciplinary Approach*, vol.1, no.1, (2014):1 – 13.

Aghamelu, Fidelis Chuka and Ejike, Emeka Cyril. "Understanding Fanon's Theory of Violence and its Relevance to Contemporary Violence in Africa." In *IGWEBUIKE: An African Journal of Arts and Humanities*, vol. 3, no.4, (2017): 22 – 44.

Ajayi, Isaac Adegboyega. "Military Regimes and Nation Building in Nigeria, 1966-1999." In *African Journal of History and Culture*, vol. 5, no 7, (2013): 138 -142.

Akinola, G. A. "Factors in the Development of a Democratic Ethics *in Africa." In Democracy, Democratization and Africa*, edited by Thomson, L.A. Ibadan: Afrika Link, (1994): 27 – 30.

Akubue, Daniel Tochukwu. *Fulfilled Dreams of Martin Lurther King Jnr: A Challenge to Nigerian Democracy*. Enugu: Ndubest Productions, 2010.

Ali, Abdweli and Is**se,** Hodan Said. "Political Freedom and Stability of Economic Policies." In Cato *Journal*, vol.24, no.3, (2005): 251 – 260.

Allesandrini, Anthony. "Introduction: Fanon Studies, Cultural Studies, Cultural Politics." In *Frantz Fanon: Critical Perspectives*, edited by Anthony Allesandrini. London: Routledge Press, (1999): 1 – 17.

Andreski, Iris. *Old Wives' Tales: Life Stories from Ibibioland*. London: Routledge and Kegan Paul.1970.

Anyadike, Nkechi."Boko Haram and National Security Challenges in Nigeria, Causes and Solutions." In *Journal of Economics and Sustainable Development*,vol. 4, no.5, (2013): 12 – 23.

Arendt, Hannah. *On Violence*. New York: Harcourt, Brace & World, 1970.

Arua, Kevin C. "Man is Free to be Free and not Free not to be Free." In *UCHE: Journal of the Department of Philosophy, University of Nigeria Nsukka*, vol.13,(2005). 1 – 13.

Audi, Robert. "On the Meaning and Justification of Violence." *In Violence: An Award Winning Essays in the Council for Philosophical Studies Competition*, edited by Jerome Shaffer, New York: David McKay Company Inc., (1971): 49 – 99.

Azar, Michael. "In the name of Algeria: Frantz Fanon and the Algerian Revolution." In *Frantz Fanon: Critical Perspectives*, edited by Anthony Allesandrini. London and New York: Routledge, 1999, (21 – 33).

Bashir, Malik Fahim and Xu, Changsheng. "Impart of Political Freedom, Economic Freedom and Political Stability on Economic Growth." In Journal *of Economics and Sustainable Development*, vol.5, no.22, (2014). 59 – 67.

Bernasconi, Robert. "Casting the Slough: Fanon's New Humanism for a New Humanity." In *Fanon: A Critical Reader*, edited by Gordon, L.R., et al. U.S.A: Blackwell Publishers Inc.,(1996): 113 – 121.

Blackburn, Simon. *Oxford Dictionary of Philosophy*. Oxford: Oxford University Press, 2008.

Bulham, Hussein Abdilahi, *Frantz Fanon and the Psychology of Oppression*. New York: Plenum Press, 1985.

Burtt, Edwin Arthur. Religion *in an Age of Sciences*. London: Williams and Norgate, 1970.

Carastathis, Anna, "Fanon on Turtle Island: Revisiting the Question of Violence." In *Fanon and the Decolonization of Philosophy*, edited by Elizabeth A. Hoppe and Tracey Nicholls, Uk: Lexington Books (2010): 77 – 102.

Caute, David. *Frantz Fanon*. New York: The Viking Press, 1970.

Cesaire Aime, "The Homage to Frantz Fanon." In *Prescence Africaine*, vol. 12, no.40, 1962.

Chinweuba, Gregory Emeka. "Low Level Corruption in Nigerian Society: A Critical Investigation." In *ORACLE OF WISDOM Journal of Philosophy and Public Affairs*, vol. 4, no. 1,(2020): 26 – 40.

_____. "Politics: The Dialectical Base of Poverty and Prosperity in Nigeria." In *Nnamdi Azikiwe Journal of Philosophy*, vol. 11, no. 2, (2019): 38 – 48.

_____. "Restructuring Nigeria: A Critical Study of its Relevance in Sustainable Development." In *Sapientia Journal of Philosophy*, vol. 10, (2019): 134 – 145.

Clarke, Harry and Summers, Lucinda. *New Webster's Dictionary of the English Language*. U.S.A: Delan Publishing Inc., 1981.

DuBois, W.E.B. *The Souls of Black Folk*. With Introduction by S. Redding, New York: Dodd, Mead & Co, 1966.

Eckstein, Harry. "Authority Patterns: A Structural Basis for Political Inquiry." In *The American Political Science Review*, vol. 67, no. 4,(1973): 1142 -1161.

Edward Said, *Culture and Imperialism*. London: Chattox Windos, 1993.

Ejiogu, E.C. "The Roots of Political Instability in Nigeria." 1 -21, accessed September 14, 2021 from: https: //wwwdocs.hsrc. ac. za. Ejiogu-the-roots-of-political-instability-in-nigeria.

Ejiofor, Peter. "Dynamics of Party Politics in Democracy: The case of Nigeria." In *Church and Democracy in West Africa : Proceedings of the Conference of the Fourteenth CIWA Theology*

Week Held at the Catholic Insistute of West Africa, Portharcourt, 7 – 11 April, 2003, edited by F. Nwigbo. Port Harcourt: CIWA Publications, 2003.

Enoch Samuel, Stumpf. *Philosophy History & Problems.* New York: McGraw-Hill, 1994.

Ene, et al. "Corruption Control and Political Stability in Nigeria: Implication for Value Re-Orientation in Politics." In *The Journal of Modern African Studies,* vol.18, no. 1,(1980): 135 – 142.

Etim, Frank O. and Ukpere, Wilfred. "The Impart of Military Rule on Democracy in Nigeria" In *Global Journal of Human Social Sciences,* vol. 13, no. 1, (2013): 7 - 12.

Fanon, Frantz. *A Dying Colonialism,* translated by Haakon Chevalier. New York: Grove Press, 1965.

_____, *Black Skin, White Masks,* translated by Charles Lan Markmann. London: Plato Press, 2008.

_____*The Wretched of the Earth,* translated by Constance Farrington. London: Penguin Books, 2001.

_____*Towards the African Revolution,* translated by Haakon Chevalier. New York: Grove Press, 1967.

Fukuyama, Francis. The *End of History and the Last Man.* New York: Penguin Books, 1992.

Gendzier, Irene. *Frantz Fanon: A Critical Study.* New York: Random House, 1973.

_____, *Frantz Fanon: A Critical Study.* London: Wild Wood House Ltd, 1972.

Gesimar, Peter. *Frantz Fanon.* New York: Dail Press, 1971.

Gordon, Lewis. "Fanon on Decolonizing knowledge." In *Fanon and the Decolonization of Philosophy,* edited by Elizabeth A. Hoppe and Tracey Nicholls (UK: Lexington Books, 2010): 3 – 17.

Guven, Ferit. "Hegel, Fanon and the Problem of Negativity in Post-Colonial." In *Fanon and the Decolonization of Philosophy,* edited by Elizabeth Hoppe and Tracey Nicholls UK: Lexington Books, 2010: 167 – 176.

Harris, Leonard and Johnson, Carolyn. "Forward." In *Fanon: A Critical Reader,* edited by Gordon, L. R. et al, U.S.A: Blackwell Publishers, 1990

Hayes, Floyd. "Fanon, Oppression and Resentment: The Black Experience in the United States." *In Fanon: A Critical Reader,* edited by Gordon, L.R., et al. U.S.A: Blackwell Publishers Inc., (1996): 11 – 23.

Hojo, James. *Nigerian Government and the Youth, What is Happening?* Orlu: Ogechi Press, 2009.

Hountondji, Paulin. African *Philosophy, Myth and Reality.* London: Hutchinson University Library for Africa, 1983.

Igboin, Benson. "Boko Haram Fundamentalism: A Critical Metamorphosis." In *CJR,* vol. 3, no.2,(2015): 72 – 97.

Igwe, Stanley C., *How Africa Underdeveloped Africa.* Port Harcourt: Prime Print Technologies, 2012.

Ikejiani-Clark, Miriam. "Governor-Generalship/Presidency of Nigeria." In *Azikiwe and the African Revolution,* edited by M.S.O Olisa and Miriam Ikejiani- Clerk. Onitsha; Africana-Fep Publishers Ltd, 1989.

Isife, Evaristus Emeka. "Dialectics of Freedom in Frantz Fanon and its Relevance in Contemporary Africa." In *IGWEBUIKE: An African Journal of Arts and Humanities*, vol. 6, no. 9,(2020): 118 – 131.

_____ "Dialectics of Freedom in Frantz Fanon: A Potent Tool towards Achieving Political Stability in Nigeria." In *The International Journal of Humanities & Social Studies* vol. 8, no.5, (2020): 265 – 272.

_____ "Political Instability in Nigeria: Causes, Impacts and Philosophic Solutions." In *AMAMIHE: Journal of Applied Philosophy*, vol. 18, no. 6,(2020): 1 – 11.

Kuhn, Thomas. "The Structure of Scientific Revolution." In *International Encyclopedia of Unified Science* edited by Otto Neurath et al. London: The University of Chicago Press Ltd, 1970.

McCulloch, Jock, *Black Soul White Artifact: Fanon's Clinical Psychology and Social Theory.* New York: Cambridge University Press, 2002.

Memmi, Albert. "Caute, Fanon and Gesmar." The *New York Times Book Review* March 14, 1971.

Meredith, Marthin. *The State of Africa.* UK: Simon and Schuster, 2011.

Muse, Sulaimon Adigun and Narsiah, Sagie. "Challenges to Public Participation in Political Processes in Nigeria." In *Journal of Social Science,*vol. 44, nos. 2,3 (2015): 181 – 187.

Ndianefoo, Ifechukwu. *A Critical History of Philosophy of Science.* Awka: Divine Press, 2016.

Nigel Gibson. "Fanon and the Pitfalls of Cultural Studies." In *Frantz Fanon: Critical Perspectives,* edited by Anthony Allesandrini. London: Routledge, (1999): 101 – 126.

Nmah, P. H. "Nigeria: Democracy, Human Rights and Niger Delta Issue." In *The Humanities and Nigeria's Democratic Experience* edited by Chiegboka, A. B.C et al. Nimo: Rex Charles & Patrick Ltd, 2009: 171 – 174.

Nnoli, O. *Ethnic Politics in Nigeria.* Enugu: Fourth Dimension Publishing Co. Ltd. 1980.

Nweke, Charles. "The Philosophy of Non-Violence and the Niger Delta Question." In Journal *of the Department of Philosophy*, Nnamdi Azikiwe University, Awka, Nigeria, vol.5, no.1 (2013): 50 -64.

Nwodo, John. Restructuring *Nigeria: Decentralization for Normal Cohesion.* Chatham House: The Royal Institute of International Affairs, 27 September, 2017.

Odey, John. *This Madness Called Election 2003.* Enugu: Snaap Press Ltd., 2003.

Odoziobodo, Severus Ifeanyi. *Society & Revolution: A Nigerian Perspective.* Enugu: Education Promotion Agency, 2003.

Ogbeidi Michael. M. "Political Leadership and Corruption in Nigeria Since 1960: A Socio-Economic Analysis." In *Journal of Nigeria Studies* 1, no. 2 (2012): 1 – 25.

Ogbu Kalu. "Tradition in Revolutionary Change." In Ikenga *Journal of African Studies* 3, nos. 1 & 2(1975): 53 – 58.

Ojiako, J.O. *Nigeria: Yesterday, Today and …?* Onitsha: African Educational Publishers Ltd., 1981.

Ojukwu, Odumegwu. *Biafra: Random Thoughts.* New York: Harper& Row, Publishers, 1969.

Okolo B. *Education and Nigerian Values: A Companion for Students.* Enugu: Cecta(Nig) Ltd. 1993.

Okoye, Darlynton. "Peace Support Organizations in Nigeria." In *Peace Studies and Conflict Resolution in Nigeria: A Reader*, edited by Miriam Ikejiani-Clark. Ibadan: Spectrum Book Ltd, (2009): 248 – 265.

Olusoji, George. "Military Interventions in the Nigeria Politics: A 'time bomb' waiting to Explode? The Avowal of a New Management Elites." In *International Journal of Business, Humanities and Technology*, vol. 2, (2012): 191 – 197.

Onah, Ikechukwu. *The Battle of Democracy: Social Justice and Punishment in Africa*. Enugu: Fidgina Global Books, 2006.

Onwuanibe, Richard. *A Critique of Revolutionary Humanism: Frantz Fanon*. U.S.A: Warren H. Green, Inc., 1983.

Orizu, Nwafor. *Without Bitterness: West Nations in Post War Africa*. Enugu: Nwaife Publishers Ltd, 1981.

Osimen, Goddy Uwa, et al. "Ethnicity and Identity Crisis: Challenge to National Integration in Nigeria." In *Journal of Humanities and Social Science*, vol. 16, Issue 4, (2013): 79 – 83.

Otu, Ato–Sekyi. *Fanon's Dialectic of Experience*. London: Harvard University Press, 1996.

Parris, La Rose T. "Frantz Fanon: Existentialist, Dialectician, and Revolutionary." In *The Journal of Pan African Studies*, vol.4, no. 7,(2011): 4 – 23.

Rabaka, Reiland. *Forms of Fanonism: Critical Theory and the Dialectics of Decolonization*. UK: Lexington Book, 2011.

Reports of the Constitutional Drafting Committee 1. Enugu: Ministry of Education and Information, 1979.

Rousseau, Jean-Jacques. *The Social Contract*, translated Maurice Cranson. England: Penguin Books, 1968.

Sartre, Jean Paul. "Ophee noir." In *Anthologie de la nouvelle poesienegre et malgache de langue Francaise*, edited by L.S. Senghor. Paris: Presses Universitaires de France, 1969.

Siollun, Max. Oil, *Politics and Violence: Nigeria Military Coup Culture: 1966-1976*, New York: Algora Publishers, 2009.

Tamdgidi, Muhamed. "Decolonizing Selves: The Subtler Violence of Colonialism and Racism in Fanon, Said and Anzaldua." In *Fanon and the Decolonization of Philosophy* Elizabeth A. Hoppe and Tracey Nicholls. UK : Lexington Books,(2011): 117 – 147.

Taylor, Charles. "What's Wrong with Negative Liberty?" In *Philosophical Papers*. Cambridge: Cambridge University Press, (2012): 211- 229.

Wright, Claudia. "National Liberation, Consciousness, Freedom and Frantz Fanon." In *History of European Ideas*, vol. 15, nos. 1-3, (1996): 427 – 434.

Zahar, Renate, *Frantz Fanon: Colonialism and Alienation*. New York: Monthly Review Press, 1974.

INDEX

Nigel Gibson 14
Niger Basin 38
Niger Delta 54-55, 66
Niger Delta Avengers (NDA) 55
Niger Delta People Volunteer Force (NDPVF) 55
Nigeria 1, 37-38, 40-53, 55-68, 70-71
Nigerian Politics 44, 50
Nigerian Polity 37, 41, 53
Njideka Odera Nnamdi 59
Nkechi Anyadike 56
Nnamdi Azikiwe 46, 50
Non-Violent Resistance 67
Northern Region 46
Nwafor Orizu 45

O

Obafemi Awolowov 46
Obasanjo 47-48, 51
Odoziobodo 40
Odumegwu Ojukwu 52
Okolo 51-52
Olusoji 49
Ontology 8
Oppression 3, 12-13, 31-32, 36, 44, 66
Osimen Goddy Uwa Et Al 61
Other 62

P

Pandemic 63
Paradigm 4, 7, 58, 68, 70
Parliamentary System of Government 46
Paulin Hountondji 22
Paulo Friere 16
Pessimism 44
Peter Geismar 14, 16
Phenomenology 17, 20
Philosophy 9, 11, 26
Philosophy of Science 4
Plato 2, 9
Political Consciousness 61
Political Culture 54
Political Freedom 54
Political Instability 5, 15, 37, 40-44, 46-49, 52, 58
Political Stability 58, 65, 68, 70
Politics 5, 13, 39, 46, 48, 50-51, 53, 62, 64-65, 70
Polity 38, 42
President Trump 63
Protectorate Government of Northern Nigeria 38

Psychoanalysis 12
Psychological Mechanism 14
Psychology 12, 32
Psychotherapeutics 18

Q

Quota System 53

R

Race 14, 28, 61
Racial Oppression 13
Racialization 3
Racism 12-14, 17, 25, 27, 66, 68
Reality 29
Reciprocity 8, 14-15, 20-21, 29
Reconciliation 53
Reiland Rabaka 17
Renate Zahar 14, 16
Resistance 31
Revelation 31
Revolution 5, 9, 31, 68
Revolutionary Fanonism 17
Revolutionary Violence 68
Richard Onwuanibe 9
Robert Bernasconi 35
Royal Military College 53

S

Sandhurst 53
Sartre 8-9, 12, 14-15, 21, 24, 26-27, 66
Saudi Arabia 56
Science 4
Self 30, 62, 70
Self/Other-Other/Self Relation 29
Self-Alienation 28
Self-Consciousness 2, 12, 20
Self-Defense 66
Self-Determination 9
Self-Other Dialectic 29
Sexism 17
Sidney Hook 16
Slavery 3
Social Consciousness 62
Social Contract 40-41
Socialist Revolution 17
Sokoto 38
Sorel Paneto 33
Subjective Method 24
Systemic Corruption 42

Printed in the United States
by Baker & Taylor Publisher Services